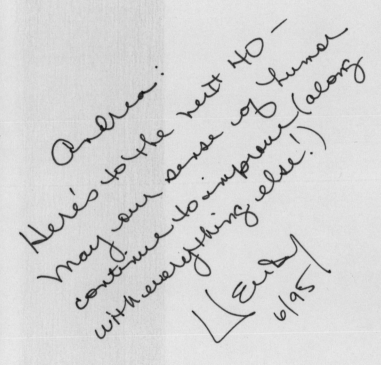

Andrea:
Here's to the next 40 —
may our sense of humor
continue to improve (along
with everything else!)

Erin
6/95

I Have Everything

I Had

Twenty Years Ago,

Except

Now It's All Lower

By the same author

The Toast Always Lands Jelly-Side Down

I Have Everything

I Had

Twenty Years Ago,

Except

Now It's All Lower

SUZANN LEDBETTER

Illustrated by Heidi Graf

Crown Publishers, Inc., New York

To Mom and Daddy, for everything

Published by Crown Publishers, Inc., 201 East 50th Street, New York, New York 10022. Member of the Crown Publishing Group.
Random House, Inc. New York, Toronto, London, Sydney, Auckland
Crown is a trademark of Crown Publishers, Inc.

Portions of this work were originally published in *Family Circle* in 1993 and 1994.

Manufactured in the United States of America

Design by Lauren Dong

Library of Congress Cataloging-in-Publication Data
Ledbetter, Suzann.
        I have everything I had twenty years ago : except now it's all lower/Suzann Ledbetter.
        I. Title.
PN6162.L358   1995
818'.5402—dc20   94-41336

ISBN: 0-517-59979-1

10 9 8 7 6 5 4 3 2 1

First Edition

Acknowledgments

Though this tome carries my byline, there's a whole lotta folks that deserve equal credit for its existence: a host of Crown Publishers staff members, including and especially my editor Jane Cavolina and publicist Julie Lovrinic, agent extraordinaire Robin Rue, *Family Circle* magazine's Susan Ungaro and Nancy Clark, plus an army of writer-friends who have been my salvation on more occasions than I can count—Paul W. Johns, Deborah Morgan (Estleman) and Loren D. Estleman, Ray Rosenbaum, Fred Bean, Dale L. Walker, Sheri McCall, Jory and Charlotte Sherman, Jim Hamilton, S. Kent Baker, W. C. Jameson, and Tri-County Feedback Group members Debbie Redford, Beth Urich, and Jim Sieger.

Last, but most of all, here's to you, Cecilia, Laurie, Josh, and Zach, who mean the world to me.

Contents

MY COUNTRY 'TIS OF THEE

IN WORKING ORDER

Me and Mine

A mother is neither cocky, nor proud, because she knows

the school principal may call any minute to report that her

child has just driven a motorcycle through the gymnasium.

MARY KAY BLAKELY

I'd Rather Be Forty Than Pregnant

'll not argue that there are any number of good reasons for procrastinating pregnancy. Establishing a career and a more sound financial footing, achieving a feeling of emotional readiness, and becoming acclimated to one's own world before bringing another person into it are laudable, common-sense inducements to keep the stork circling for a few years.

But whenever a talk show features forty-something, first-time mothers, *I* get cold chills.

Experience is the best teacher. Hindsight is twenty-twenty. And both give ample reason for glee that I'm in motherhood's semifinals instead of anticipating the first heat.

Though Younger Son delights in calling me a geezer, I'm far from ready to be put out to pasture. But I have to admit, this graying mare ain't what she used to be. As Gypsy Rose Lee once quipped, "I have everything I had twenty years ago, except now it's all lower"—nor can I deny that it works considerably slower.

I've always wondered why the predelivery process is called "labor." Birthing a baby *is* done lying down, with any number of medical assistants' help, and drugs are available upon request.

It's a day or two postpartum, when Mom's on her own, when the *real* labor begins. It doesn't matter that her sitter-downer still kinda smarts because she won't get many opportunities to use it for the next couple of decades anyhow.

In retrospect, I'd compare child raising to pushing a '58 Edsel, in first gear, with a jammed emergency brake and a Sumo wrestling team on board, from New York to Honolulu—and back.

Despite Dad's willingness to share child care responsibilities, a baby can cry "Momma" months before "Dada" stutters forth, and I always felt compelled to answer my page personally.

During those first months of motherhood, I assumed that if there were any other adults roaming around in the wee-houred darkness, they'd probably just robbed a convenience store. A good night's sleep was but a memory. A good hour's *nap* would have been a dream, and I thoroughly enjoyed the two I got while my four kids were growing up.

Their sleep-through-the-night status was well established before mine believed all was truly well and kicked in accordingly. And I certainly needed that snooze time since their ability to crawl came next, and achieved four-on-the-floor warp speed about thirty-seven hours before they started walking. Then running. Away from me.

As toddlers, they were instinctively attracted to toxic chemicals, small swallowable objects, heights, depths, electrical outlets, stairways, door handles, and puddles.

Conversely, they were repelled by vegetables, naps, wearing shoes (but not gnawing on them), nose wiping, repeating new vocabulary words to anyone other than me and Dad, and all public displays of inherently sunny dispositions.

Almost overnight came the ability to go potty (but not flush) and dress themselves (snowsuits in July and beachwear in January), as well as socialization skills, including becoming best friends with the only kid in North America who could choose his/her own bedtime, meal menus, playtime activities, and had an aisle named in his/her honor at the local Toys "Я" Us.

Little did I know that when my kids' adolescent hormones started rising like tree sap, those incredibly physically and emotionally demanding preceding years would seem like a holiday in St. Croix.

Just as in infancy, my teenagers got their days and nights mixed up, which meant innumerable sleep-deprived encores for me. Like babies, adolescents are constantly hungry, too. Although with age should come the capability to feed themselves, mine were known to flounder helplessly in the kitchen as if their arms were just *painted* on.

I began to suspect that their legs were, too, when they suddenly refused to walk or bike anywhere. If car keys or a ride couldn't be begged, they just didn't go, but did let me know that by being *so* selfish, I was pretty much *ruining* their lives.

Scientists haven't located them yet, but I'm convinced that teenagers have a set of Surly Glands which go from dormancy to overdrive during puberty. With Surly Gland function comes the attitude that Mom and Dad are prime examples of nonintelligent life forms, and that peers are supremely insightful, money grows on trees, and curfews are made to be broken.

That I survived that stage *three times* during my twenties and thirties is enough to make me believe in miracles. With the last of my lot's pubescent uprising still to come in my forties, that "Over the Hill" slogan painted on my coffee cup gains greater significance every day.

From a purely hindsighted perspective, thoughts of starting the parenting process midlife, with adolescent growing uppityness duly arriving in my late fifties and sixties seems the stuff Stephen King's plots are made of.

Now that I've also reached grandmotherdom—a distinction, I'll admit, I'd have delayed if I'd been allowed a vote on the subject—simply *watching* my twenty-something daughters trying to keep up with their respective toddlers is enough to make *me* need a nap.

Younger Son may say I'm a geezer already, but words cannot sufficiently express how delighted I am that I'll be *out* of the PTA before I'm even *eligible* to join the AARP.

Home Is the Sailor . . .

A rancher friend puts goldfish in his livestock watering tanks every winter to keep the water from freezing. He doesn't feed them—pays no attention to them at all. And the critters not only survive, they're pan-sized by spring.

In my subdivision, installing a stock tank in the backyard would be met with the same neighborly enthusiasm as acquiring a herd of the actual cattle for which that trough was intended. So, when my children had a hankering for some finned friends, I went whole hog: a fifty-five-gallon aquarium with a fluorescently lighted lid, a filtration system, bags of multicolored rocks, a miniature pirate ship to rest on said rocks, and several clumps of plastic greenery.

Once the equipment was operational, the children and I purchased a pair of goggle-eyed goldfish. For no rational reason, the new owners named their pets Lucky and Steve.

Two days later, Steve was still swimming laps around the scuttled pirate ship, as he did about nine hundred and forty-one times per hour, but Lucky was floating belly-up at the top of the tank.

I expected my kids to insist upon a backyard funeral as they had for various domesticated rodents who'd met similar fates. The next century's archaeologists may be hard-pressed to explain how the fossils they'll find at our former homesite got sealed inside Pringles tubes and Band-Aid tins.

Thankfully, the children hadn't had time to "bond" with Lucky and thought the toilet-style burial at sea I suggested was an appropriate send-off for their aquatic acquaintance.

Following the service, we returned to the pet store for a replacement so Steve wouldn't get lonesome. Before I got Steve's roommate flopped into the tank, it had been duly christened Lucky II.

Lucky II was the same size Lucky I had been. Lucky II even sported a tiny white patch on its back in about the same spot Lucky I had. The only difference between Lucky I and Lucky II was that the latter lasted *four* days before departing for that Big Aquarium in the Sky.

Worse yet, Steve went with him.

The children were slightly more solemn during the two-flush ceremony for Lucky II and Steve. "Here he lies where he longs to be," I recited for the second time in a week. "Home is the sailor, home from the sea."

Between stanzas, I couldn't help wondering whether Robert Louis Stevenson had been similarly inspired when he penned those "mortal" lines. Nor could I help wondering what such frequent deposits of gone-but-not-forgotten fin pals were doing to our septic system.

Although the fish we'd picked obviously lacked a never-say-die attitude, the family was all for try, try again.

Lucky III and Steve, Jr., were toted home in a water-filled plastic bag the next day—and went out with the tide a week later.

Lucky IV and Steve III checked out after only one night.

Why remained a mystery. I'd done everything possible to ensure those fish an ecologically correct, stable environment. Rather than believe myself to be the world's first serial gold-fish killer, I decided I simply had a knack for picking oxygen-challenged pets.

Leaving the tank empty seemed like a good idea until I remembered how much money I'd already invested. That kind of reasoning is comparable to spending $196.43 on car repairs simply because I'd already shelled out $103.87 two months earlier to fix a different malfunction, making the old flivver too valuable to part with.

Since frequent purchases had put me on a first-name basis with the fish department's salesperson, I called her for clues to the cause of these small-scale fish kills.

When overfeeding, overdoses of chlorine, and the possibility of the aquarium's heater being accidentally cranked up to parboil were ruled out, we were both stumped.

Despite the unprecedented, unsolved death rate, the kids

were clamoring for some semblance of marine life to watch besides the algae growing up the glass and air bubbles burbling up the filter tubes.

I agreed, conditionally: This time, I insisted that (a) the fish would remain nameless until they survived a complete moon phase, and (b) under no circumstances would they then be tagged Lucky or Steve—with or without numerals.

It was obvious the moment we arrived at the fish department that the dozens on display *knew* we'd already flushed six of their cousins. Like an alarm had sounded, they immediately turned belly-up, faking the now-familiar Dead-Fish Float.

Every few seconds, as if one had asked, "Are they gone yet?" a mottled specimen bobbing near the front of the tank peered at me through a slightly opened eyelid, then sneaked it shut again.

As one fish after another gave up playing possum, it joined other potential homicide victims cowering behind a ceramic deep-sea diver statuette.

Because the last pair to resuscitate themselves had proven their survival instinct, we bagged 'em, bought 'em, and hoped like heck we wouldn't soon be burying 'em.

Many months have passed and I'm pleased to report that those fine finned friends are getting along swimmingly. However, choosing their names did prove a tad tricky.

It was decided that Gill and Goldie was a skosh too cutesy. Hekyl and Jekyl was for the birds. Spouse suggested The Naked and The Damned, but that just wouldn't do for a G-rated ownership.

The monikers we settled on are hard for the children to pronounce and even tougher to spell, but so far, the fish are living up to their good names: Methuselah and Geezer.

In fact, at the rate they're snarfing food flakes, they just may be pan-sized by spring.

Facial Faux Pas

$\mathcal{S}$hortly after sort-of celebrating my fortieth birthday, I noticed that when Younger Son said, "Gee, Mom, you don't look *that* old," an unspoken but definite "yet" dangled at the end of it.

Now to my mind, any mother of four who doesn't have any wrinkles to show for it has probably either had them surgically removed, or has been in a coma for a couple of decades. But it's also true that I've never thought crow's feet were particularly attractive on *crows*.

Fearing a rapid advancement to the "you look *fine* for a woman your age" stage of life, I decided that a session with a professional cosmetician might slow my inevitable advance into crone-ism, somewhat.

Although I'm sure our nation boasts millions of unthreateningly average-looking makeup artists, naturally, the gal who greeted me could have been Cindy Crawford's prettier sister and had obviously never suffered a bad *anything* day.

There are few things more depressing than asking for cosmetic advice from someone who probably isn't old enough to wear makeup and definitely doesn't need it, anyway. But, since I'd already told everyone except CNN to expect the debut of an enticing "New Me," there was no turning back.

My first lesson was how to properly wash my face—a twice-daily regimen I was astounded to find out could actually be done *wrong*.

Rather than slathering on whatever soap was handy and then splashing it off with enough water to soak me to my socks, I was told to smear on a coat of cleansing cream, then wipe off gently with a washcloth rotating in precise, counter-clockwise circles.

This method not only required concentrated coordination, it took a heck of a lot longer than my traditional technique: squinching my eyes closed, aiming handfuls of water in the general direction of my face, then groping blindly for the nearest towel.

Once I'd been stripped of all cosmetic camouflage, Ms. Cosmetician slid a turkey platter–sized magnifying mirror in front of me. The immediate realization that my amplified reflection closely resembled a bas-relief map of Utah did nothing to boost my self-esteem.

Choosing and applying foundation was another procedure more complicated than I'd imagined. Instead of grabbing whichever shade of the forty-three half-full bottles in my bathroom drawer that rolled to the front fastest, the cosmetician scrutinized me for several minutes to determine what kind of skin I had.

While I'd always thought "cruddy" pretty much summed it up, she diagnosed my complexion as "basically, combination." However, she added, quite somberly, that my "oily T-zone" would require extra attention.

I wasn't aware that I *had* a T-zone, let alone where it was or how to fix it, so I just sat back and let her daub my forehead, nose, cheeks, and chin with a stings-like-hell astringent. And I don't know whether my T-zone shaped up as a result or not, but all eight sinus passages cleared in about five seconds flat.

With my face a shiny, clockwise clean, and my T-zone fried into submission, I was deemed sufficiently prepped for "New Me" maneuvers. Because I've worn makeup for more years than my mother is aware of, I thought I had finally reached familiar territory. Of course, I'd thought I'd had a handle on face washing since I got tall enough to reach the sink, too.

While shaking a bottle of the prescribed "Combination II—X-tra-Strength Venusian Taupe," Ms. Cosmetician stressed that foundation should always be applied using the ring finger *only*. Although she conceded that my custom of troweling it on with as many fingers as would fit on my face was faster, such heavy-handed smearing not only contributed to wrinkle production, it left behind a sort-of stucco effect that was a scootch shy of natural looking.

Until that moment, I had no idea that my ring finger was good for anything besides displaying jewelry. And in my case, it isn't. Dabbling on liquid make-up with that weak, nondextrous digit was akin to oil painting with an overboiled hot dog.

Brushloads of blusher lent a rosy, diptherialike glow to my cheekbones, followed by an overall, gale-force "dusting" of loose powder to "set" all of the above.

After being informed that my "small eyes" simply cried out for cosmetic enlargement, Ms. Cosmetician asked if I'd just close them and let her work her magic, sight unseen.

"When I get through with you, you won't *believe* the difference. You'll be absolutely *stunning*," she promised.

About fifteen minutes later, when I opened my eyes, by golly, I really *couldn't* believe the difference.

I'd started the session looking like a typical middle-aged,

undermadeup, chronically overtired female. But with swashes of Midnight Ebony shadow, heavy strokes of Jet Raven eye-liner striping my top and bottom lids, and enough layers of Bituminous Sable mascara to effect a decidedly semiconscious droop, I'd been transformed, *unbelievably*, into a dead ringer for Rory Raccoon.

All things considered, I gave Ms. Cosmetician credit for curing the various facial faux pas I'd been committing for years. And some of the make-up tips she suggested really did create a smoother, more youthful "look." Except she was only *half*-right about my reaction to her swash-stripe-and-glop eye-enlargement technique.

Despite her good intentions, believe me, the expression on the face of the black-eyed Suzann staring back from the mirror looked a whole lot closer to *stunned* than *stunning*.

Stubbling Through Life

I've never had much sympathy when Hubby complained about the facial shaving *ordeal* he suffers daily. Not when those remarks come from a mustachioed male who can, with absolute social acceptability, sport veritable thatches of hair over the remaining 98 percent of his body.

Conversely, I, being female, have only two allowable hair zones: on my head, and an anatomical region somewhat farther south—and there only when swimsuits aren't in season.

That means I'm shaving some part of my personhood darned near daily, too, and the regions that require it are a heck of a lot less accessible, not to mention more "delicate," than a man's piddlin' piece of face.

Since exiting a bathtub containing shaving cream glops and a kazillion stubble nits floating atop the water has never made me feel particularly clean, I'm a shower shaver. But because the stall is much narrower than my legs are long, I must perform flamingolike contortions while wielding a razor sharp enough to plane at least two layers of skin from my shins and knees, while leaving the hair growing there virtually unscathed.

I'm not particularly fond of the sight of blood, especially my own, but if I ever did do something serious to myself while shaving—such as "nick" a femoral artery—I'd faint from the *loss* of blood before I'd have a chance to faint from the *sight* of it.

To my knowledge, no building contractor has ever given a moment's thought to installing ceiling lights in shower stalls so the 52 percent of the population who literally risk life and limb defoliating legs, underarms, and you-know-wheres could see what the hell they're *doing* while they're *doing* it.

After too many years of in-the-dark blade shaving followed by toilet paper body wraps to stanch the flow of type O leaking from a few thousand self-inflicted wounds, I bought a bottle of chemical hair remover. Banners on its packaging not only promised to remove unwanted hair easily and efficiently, but to retard its regrowth.

My American know-how attitude precluded reading the directional sections that listed precautions and advised skin patch pretesting, so I skipped straight to the "how to apply" and "for how long" parts.

After giving the bottle a couple of jostles that probably met the "Shake well before using" instruction, I slathered the stuff on from anklebone to thigh, and was about knee-high on the other leg when, naturally, the telephone rang.

Like most mothers, I immediately assumed it was a school nurse in need of my permission before doing a Heimlich maneuver or cardiopulmonary resuscitation on one of my children. Tottering hastily to the phone and finding instead a neighborly caller on the other end, I wedged the receiver between my ear and my right shoulder and finished basting myself with depilatory.

Had a burglar chosen that moment to break in and enter my house, I'm sure his account of finding a naked woman

talking on the telephone, with her arms raised like a chicken's wings, and with what looked like lemon cake frosting smeared all over her legs, would keep his fellow inmates in stitches for weeks.

By the time I could gracefully bow out of the conversation, I was sure I'd exceeded the directional suggestion, "*Do not leave on skin longer than fifteen minutes.*" But, I figured if fifteen minutes promised an acceptable dethatching, the twenty or so that had elapsed would make those fiendish follicles think twice about *ever* growing back again.

Assuming the goop would rinse off in the shower like soap-suds, I was surprised to find it pretty much impervious to water. Then, when I bent over to scrub it off my legs with my hands, a veritable wall of drippy head-hair flopped over my face.

Without thinking, I raised up and slicked back the offending tresses, instantly realizing that by doing so, I'd finger combed a coat of depilatory chemicals through hair I most *definitely* didn't want to part with.

As I finished a second shampoo to ensure I'd removed all the accidentally applied remover, I became acutely aware of a stinging, itching, strafed-by-a-flamethrower sensation emanating from my legs and underarms. I can safely estimate it took all of two seconds—tops—to rinse off the rest of me.

Though the experience temporarily rendered those areas hairless (albeit a tad tender) a Fact of Female Life was made very clear: On my head, the one place where I *want* hair to grow thick and fast, it doesn't and never will. Those regions where I *don't* want it to grow at all are doomed to take on peltlike proportions in mere days, so whether it's done with a razor, wax, or chemical cremes, *no* kind of unwanted-hair removal process is anywhere near permanent.

Except, perhaps, scalping the next guy who gripes about having to shave his piddlin' piece of face—and leaves the bathroom sink plastered with whisker snips after he *does* it.

MST = Male Standard Time

*C*ontrary to popular opinion, chivalry is *not* dead—it's alive and well, and as close as next door.

Until a few years ago when Older Son shoveled a neighbor's driveway while ours retained knee-deep conditions for days, I hadn't realized that to those of the male persuasion, what's a "chore" at home is considered a "favor" if done elsewhere. And while the favor-provider's response time rivals paramedics en route to a Code Blue, on their own turf, honey-dos (as in "Honey, do this," or "Honey, do that") get done on Male Standard Time.

Unlike central or mountain time, Male Standard Time's boundaries aren't bold lined on a telephone book's zone map, primarily because it's common from coast to coast.

Nor is Male Standard Time something a wife can set her watch by—a calendar, maybe, as long as it's of the sixteen-month variety and she's optimistic by nature.

As most women will attest, men have a completely different (*read:* slower than molasses in January) timetable for accomplishing errands, household chores, and outings with the kiddies. However, this deviation has less to do with sexism than it does with difference in priorities.

For example, I can prepare a meal, check a homework assignment, discuss carpool options by telephone with a neighbor, supervise a backyard full of screaming children, and load the dishwasher—practically simultaneously. But the estimated time for any of the males in my family to complete the same feats ranges from two weeks to until the Twelfth of Never.

In accordance with Male Standard Time, a mention of most everything from big jobs like house painting or extensive yard work to piddly projects such as shopping for Son's new tennie-runners or changing a light bulb, results in one of the following responses:

> *"I'll get to it in a minute . . ."*
> *"Soon as the game's over . . ."*
> *"I'm just waiting for the weather to warm up a bit . . ."*
> *"Soon as I get some other stuff done . . ."*
> *"Later . . ."*
> *"Next weekend, I promise . . ."*
> *"I've gotta shake this cold, first . . ."* (Cough, cough)
> *"Aw, c'mon, lemme relax for a few minutes, will ya?"*

All of the above can be translated as, "When I get good and ready," "Perhaps, during this lifetime," or "When hell freezes over," depending on how often the requestee is willing to nag before stomping off and doing the job *herself*. Which is what Mr. Make Excuses was counting on in the first place.

Oddly enough, Male Standard Time can achieve warp speed when the matter at hand is desire oriented. Such watch-my-dust occasions include an invitation to play golf, meeting amigos for a brewski at the local watering hole, or finding Himself fifteen miles from home and five minutes from an NFL opening kickoff.

The aforementioned "favor factor" also turbo charges a he's assistance when helping a friend move, adding a room to his house, dropping a new transmission into the old pickup, or getting the boss "off the hook" by finishing a sales report due at 8 A.M. sharp, on Monday.

Without a doubt, more land-speed records have been set by men zooming off to aid and abet any of the above than on Utah's famous Salt Flats.

However, with a lot of help from similarly frustrated females in my neighborhood, we finally finagled a way to beat the boys' Male Standard Time clock. Although some might view our scheme as a conspiracy, we prefer to think of it as good old Yankee ingenuity.

Knowing our guys were always quick to respond to a woman's plea for assistance—as long as it wasn't their own mother or dearly beloved doing the plea-ing—we shes set up a secret, favor-rotation system.

If, for example, Doris, or Betty, or Frieda asks Son or Hubby to tack up a droopy downspout, rototill a garden spot, or deliver Junior to basketball practice, I get to return the "favor" by calling neighbor Bill, or Bob, or Michael to clear a stopped-up drain or adjust the garage door opener so it *will*.

Naturally, such damsel-in-distress assistance is cheerfully given so chores that have gone begging for months are getting done. And so far, none of the fellas have gotten wise to our *brilliant* manipulation of Male Standard Time.

While our methods are a smidge on the sneaky side, it's also proof that chivalry didn't go out with powdered wigs and knee pants. To paraphrase an old joke, I think there's a Sir Walter Raleigh in every man—but to get him out, you've gotta give him *time*.

I Didn't Know How Much I'd
Miss Her 'Til She Left Me

*b*est I can figure, bad hair days occur three hundred and sixty-five times per year. Good hair days are like unicorns: I may acknowledge their potential existence but have never seen one (except on someone else).

A moment's pause for a bit of subtraction is needed before I can rattle off my children's ages, but the date of my first bad hair day is permanently affixed in my memory: October 19, 1963.

That morning, getting ready for my fifth grade's school picture session coincided with my mother's decree that my bangs had hidden "my sweet face" for too long. She insisted that I wear a headband to start "training" them into backward submission.

Not only was this my first exposure to the expanse of skin called my forehead, it introduced me to the concept that items of feminine apparel could be used to "train" physical attributes.

Once this tonsorial tourniquet was in place, the resulting combination of scraggly bang ends sticking up like tail feathers, crowning a pair of rhinestone-winged, blue-framed glasses assured my sweet-faced acceptance into the Geek Hall of Fame.

During the '92 presidential campaign when Hillary Clinton started sporting a headband, I couldn't help but wonder if her mother had made a similar "sweet face" pronouncement. And photo opportunities, whether they're nightly-news-worthy or contained within a school picture packet, means Mom will find out if the Banded One cheats by stuffing the strap into her purse as soon as she's out of sight.

I was in high school before I'd regained control of my coiffure, and wore it in the requisite, late-sixties style: a pouffily ratted, shoulder-length flip.

What I wanted, and went to great lengths to achieve was "Crowning Glory." What I got is better described as "Roots of All Evil."

To create that virtual hair helmet, glops of a gelatinous substance known as Dippity Doo had to be slimed over each carefully parted hair section before rolling it around an empty frozen orange juice can, which was secured by enormous, mutant bobby pins driven into my scalp and, possibly, my brain.

Whenever I emerged from my bedroom looking like Gunga-Tin From The Planet Zirko, my father laughed so hard he almost split his Sansabelts, but what did he know?

Seventeen magazine, the beauty bible of the acne-prone, had promised that such measures would "add body and bounce to even the straightest hair."

That my body had no bounce after numerous nights spent with rows of beverage containers clamped to my skull didn't matter as long as my hairdo *did*. And it did, perfectly, on any given Sunday afternoon when I was grounded to my room.

With adulthood came a succession of stylists hired to tame my tendrils into some semblance of fashionable shape. I even provided magazine photos of Farrah Fawcett-Majors, Candice Bergen, and whatever lusciously locked movie/television star I wanted to be transformed into, to simplify the process.

That I left these sessions at least thirty dollars poorer and looking like (a) a taller version of my six-year-old self after Aunt Maxine gave me a Toni, (b) a facsimile of Beauty Shop Monthly's cover girl, or (c) Mick Jagger in drag, convinced me that I had an unerring ability to choose hairpersons who sheared sheep in the off-season.

Admittedly, since that fifth-grade headband fiasco, I've been seriously picky about my bangs—which returned to their sweet-face-hiding position the instant I got taller than my mother. But the term trim, even when accompanied by specific instructions for precise posttrim bang length, was invariably misconstrued as permission for a no-holds-barred whackfest.

The results were either a skimpy fringe reminiscent of Mamie Eisenhower or, following a spritz of a super glue–like substance, the sheep shearer/stylist employed a pronged brush and blow dryer to sculpt what appeared to be a clump of fossilized seaweed perching atop my eyebrows.

Now, before my commentary sets off slings and arrows from thousands of outraged, professional, customer-obedient hairstylists, please note that I know you're out there, somewhere, albeit nowhere near here.

And I'm extremely respectful of your hard-learned skills and compassionate attitude. Those who have left my hair looking as though it were styled with an electric lawn trimmer and answered my every "It's too damned short!" shriek with a soothing, "Now don't worry, sweetie, it'll grow out in a month or two" are certainly in the minority.

In fact, as proof that even a blind sow can find an acorn once in a while, after countless Haircuts from Hell, I eventually stumbled upon Shirley, the beautician of my dreams. From my first appointment, Shirley gave me the look I'd most desired: pretty much me, only better.

She didn't make me feel like a hair abuser for buying discount-store house-brand shampoo and conditioner instead of her salon's sixteen-bucks-a-bottle variety, or give me grief for letting those every-six-week trims stretch to ten weeks apart. And not once did she raise her eyes heavenward as if Divine Intervention were required to remedy my bumper crop of split ends.

Best of all, after a cut and style à la Shirley, I didn't feel compelled to rush home and rewash and redry my hair—a feminine tendency men consider literally throwing good money down the drain.

I can't say I achieved one of those mythical good hair days despite five years of Shirley's tender, loving care, but the truly bad ones when nothing short of a bag over my head would get me out of the house, were fewer and farther between.

That's why, when Shirley announced her betrothal to a Texan and their relocation to the Lone Star State, my state of misery inspired me to write a country-style, love-'em-and-leave-'em song.

Once I finish adding some actual lyrics to the title, I know

Reba, Wynonna or even Lyle Lovett can hit the top of the charts with, "I Didn't Know How Much I'd Miss Her 'Til She Left Me."

I'll admit, I'm having a little trouble with a stanza describing my latest post-Shirley "trim." But once I find a few more lines that rhyme with "Surly, with the Fringe on Top," I just know it'll be a million seller.

The Empire Strikes Back

The nation's best-known designers recently sponsored a televised debut of their latest clothing collections. While a moderator gushily described the ensembles, stickpersons rumored to be of the female persuasion slouched along the runway dressed in various "drop dead" wood-nymph-like garbs—none of which I'd be caught dead *in*.

Some of the "hottest" numbers were actually just reruns from the sixties. If only the couturiers had consulted their high school yearbooks, they'd have realized how dorky those duds were the first time around.

Woe was me to see that Empire waists are *in* again because even the passage of a quarter century hasn't boosted my bustline beyond a mere principality. Though I might be tempted to flaunt it, if I had it, why should I draw attention to the fact that I still don't? And, speaking as one who unfondly remembers too many months spent in similarly styled maternity frocks, darned if I'll buy clothes that make me look pregnant when I'm *not*.

Besides designs that were more attractive on hangers than

on humans, many of the garments buttoned or zipped at the *back*. Suffice it to say, there's nothing that better illustrates the body's inherent lack of limberness than a jumpsuit with a neckline-to-heinie zipper.

Men think one of the world's biggest mysteries is why, when out on the town, women rarely go to the rest room alone. The *real* mystery is why we repeatedly buy outfits that require Houdini-like escapes and can't be redonned without assistance and/or a black belt in yoga.

While watching the program, I pondered whether my low-fashion attitude came from a social calendar that's short on glamour and long on school activities, fast food dining, carpools, and K mart. During any given week, there just isn't much call for jungle-print, see-through chiffon ensembles or glittery, two-piece spandex jammies much like Mister Spock wore on "Star Trek."

Besides a somber funeral suit, a wedding guest dress, and a couple of multipurpose outfits, my closet's contents have always consisted primarily of jeans and boots.

Years ago, with a thundering herd to trailboss, jeans proved themselves the most versatile, durable duds available. Because jeans had as many pockets as I had children putting stuff in them, there was plenty of room for stray lock blocks, change from a partially spent allowance, a couple of barrettes, G.I. Joe's AK-47, Barbie's sandals, a stubby crayon, and enough bank suckers to keep everyone quiet while we shopped.

The inventory within often pooched my hipline to dual bowling bag proportions, but my purse certainly stayed a lot cleaner.

Denim is also wonderfully durable, a major fringe benefit since I never knew what was coming up next: an afternoon at the park, resprocketing a bicycle chain, an emergency room zoom for Daughter's jumped-off-the-swing-set-because-she-thought-she-could-fly stitches, or Younger Son's too-quickly-gobbled breakfast.

Whether permanently splotched with bicycle grease, blood, or recycled bacon bits, jeans, like fine wine, age gracefully. Losing a pair of favorites to an irreparable rip or the ravages of time is like losing a page from the family album.

Boots can be counted on to carry the wearer comfortably many a mile and over any kind of terrain. And to my mind, cloppy heels sound more assertive than timid tickety-ticks. When called upon to "squish that bug a'fore it *bites* me, Mommy!" believe me, there's no more potent insecticide than a solid chunk of cowhide.

Later on, those loftier heels gave me a (temporary) edge over Older Son's rampaging growth spurt. Lacking that lift, I had to look up to lay down the law, which made me feel like a dachshund taking umbrage at a Doberman.

Such cowpersonish haute couture rarely raised eyebrows in my bovine-advantaged region. Around here, boots and jeans are as common as, well, cow piles. However a couple of years ago, when the concierge at a swanky Manhattan hotel aimed a disparaging squint at my pointy-toed Justins and boot-cut britches, I felt like a Clampett on hiatus from Beverly Hills.

No doubt, if that hostelry's head honcho saw the frocks featured during that fashion show's finale, he was probably as surprised as I was. Before my very eyes, a slew of skinnies glided forth decked in concho-belted jeanery, snap-front shirts, boots, and Stetsons.

Rather than being contentedly and chronically out of style—which *is* my style—suddenly, I'm on the cutting edge of fashion mavenhood. And how quickly I've learned how pricey popularity can be.

Virtually overnight, the going rate for four-pocket denims shot from $20 to $50 or more. A similar inflationary spiral kicked the price of even the plainest pair of boots into the stratosphere. Faster than those matchstick models could yodel "Yeehaw," *anything* that could conceivably be called "Western" got a couple of zeros added to its price tag.

Due to this unfortunate economic upsurge, the consumer price index won't be gaining any points from my pocketbook for a while, but eventually, like leisure suits and bell bottoms, this fashion phase, too, shall pass.

But when that designer-labeled, country-style haute couture does ride off into the trendy sunset, and every store stuck with veritable bales of cape-backed shirts and fancy-stitched jeans starts flying enormous CLOSEOUT SALE banners, I'll be the first in line when the doors open.

And I'll clop straight for the "collection" bearing my favorite designer names: Drastically Reduced and Clearance.

Birthday Boondoggles

Children's birthday parties are hardly the cake 'n' ice cream, frilly dress, Mary Janes, and Pin the Tail on the Donkey affairs they once were.

In the first place, today's soirees must revolve around a theme, and be it Barney, Batman, or Barbie, everything from the invitations to the cake decoration has to match. The one time I tried to economize with plain white paper plates and brown lunch sacks for loot bags, that ghastly breach of Proper Party Procedure almost got the guest of honor banished from preschool story time, forever.

Thankfully, most of the pricier paper goods come in packages of eight—I refuse to buy more than one package—which prevents the birthday child from inviting everyone she's ever said hello to during her lifetime.

But regardless of whether it was a son's or a daughter's special day we were celebrating, the aftermath of an at-home party invariably left my living room with a decidedly *Raid on Entebbe* ambiance.

On one occasion, after risking the rupture of several arteries by blowing up a huge cluster of balloons, the kids had every one of them popped in about seven and a half seconds. Not only did the noise convince me that Edwin Hubble's big bang theory was undoubtedly inspired by one of *his* kid's birthday parties, I was left with nothing to show for all my efforts besides what looked like a multicolored swarm of shriveled, string-tied navels.

Even if I controlled the partiers' urge to use the bookcases for a jungle gym, the furniture for a trampoline, or the floor for a wrestling mat, I never found an acceptable food or drink that blended with my carpet's color when it got spilled and then thoroughly, and repeatedly, squished into the fibers.

Games also posed a problem: pieces that could either be hurled, swallowed, broken, used as torture devices, or strewn from one end of the house to the other, *were*. And if prizes were awarded, there was always one kid who won *every* round of *every* game, which sent all the other players into crying, foot-stomping snits. Diplomatically changing the rules to reward the last-placer didn't work either. The same child was just as adept at losing the competition as he'd been at winning it.

Children also have a natural herding instinct and there's nothing like a birthday party to bring it out. For example, no sooner would one swipe on a chocolate icing mustache, than I'd find myself surrounded by a gaggle of giggling Groucho Marxes. That wouldn't have been so bad if it hadn't inspired war painting each other's faces with any available substance that would stick, or better yet, leave indelible stains.

For the same reason, renting an action-adventure movie to entertain the troops turned out to be a major mistake. Instead of sitting quietly and watching the show as I'd hoped, several started acting out what they saw on the screen by wielding the fireplace tools like swords while using the sofa cushions for shields.

Because too many of these annual events were more akin to indoor demolition derbies than parties, I thought holding the next scheduled celebration at a restaurant that catered to kids was a dandy idea. Unfortunately, the adjacent diners got a tad testy when pizza slices started flying through the air like shrapnel.

And it proved impossible to keep five hyperactive little girls from running under, over, around, and through the table legs while simultaneously checking on the three who had wandered off to the rest room fifteen minutes earlier and not yet returned.

While I did send a scout to report on the bathroom brigade, *that* resulted in my having *four* munchkins holed up in the potty instead of three.

As a last resort, I started emphasizing the fun instead of the food. If for no other reason, it seemed reasonable to assume that pooping out the partygoers would markedly improve their behavior.

Too late I learned that putting a crew of kids behind six-pound bowling balls, or on skates, or in possession of steel-headed miniature golf clubs was just *asking* for paramedic intervention.

Dumb luck eventually resolved many of these birthday boondoggles: by the time my kids got the stupendous idea of hosting a sleepover, I was fresh out of alternative ideas.

Comparatively speaking, these totally misnamed "slumber parties" proved pretty successful as long as a few rules were followed:

• Friday night only, so school attendance would (hope-fully) take some of the edge off the invitees' energy reserves.

The invitations also stated that any child not picked up by 10 A.M. sharp on Saturday would be sold or would have to help clean up the wreckage.

- A portion of the party budget must be set aside to cover postparty carpet shampooing, icing glop removal, and any other domestic damages incurred, plus the cost of any prescription medication prescribed for the host's mother as part of her recovery from the event.

- If the noise level and/or sneaking out for a spot of minor vandalism caused the neighbors to call the police, the posting of bail was each child's own bailiwick. That a perpetrator's last name matched mine would be dismissed as merely a coincidence.

Unfortunately, now that myriad experiences have made me a seasoned, savvy veteran, most of my children have reached the age when all they want is a pickup load of chips, dip, and cola, and for me to make myself scarce during boy-girl bashes held in our *very* dark, *very* quiet basement.

And while I'm upstairs wondering, for the one million nine hundred seventy thousandth time what the *heck's* going *on* down there and not at all sure I *really* want to know, I can't help wishing that I had nothing more to worry about than a living room full of hyperactive, chocolate mustachioed, sugar-crazed six-year-olds.

Freaky Clean

With four kids in residence, I learned long ago that cleanliness isn't next to godliness. It's next to impossible. In fact, maintaining a consistent level of benign neglect often demands more energy than I possess.

Contrary to the opinion of certain relatives whose names I won't mention (but may drop from my will), it simply isn't true that the only time I cook "decent" meals or clean the house is when guests are expected.

My casual attitude toward regular home maintenance and food preparation merely reflects a preference for the Lived-in Look and menus anchored by casseroles, meat loaf, and home-delivered pizza.

However, I will admit, there's something about inviting friends over that does make me want to spruce up the abode a bit.

On these occasions, Standard Operating Procedure means I'll dust and vacuum the "guest" rooms only. If later a whole-house tour is suggested, the merest hint that a child is upstairs recovering from bubonic plague almost always results in a postponement.

After scouring the bathrooms, I'll perk up the place by dropping a makes-the-water-blue canister in the toilet tank and putting out the monogrammed towel set and shell-shaped soaplets that were given as a Christmas gift in 1978 and never yet used, by anyone, much less the guests they're supposed to impress.

Policing the Perimeter follows, which includes emptying overflowing wastebaskets and picking up all rebounded paper and tissue wads that simply lacked the gumption to leap from the floor and launch *themselves* into the aforementioned receptacles.

After bundling all magazines and newspapers dating back to the previous presidential administration, I'll toss them into a dark corner of the garage alongside the ever-increasing collection of empty beverage cans. During this lifetime, I may even schlepp *all* of the above to an actual recycling center, but not on the day guests are due to arrive.

That routine does neaten the nest appreciably, only somehow, when company's coming, it suddenly just doesn't seem like *enough*. Instead of a satisfied shift into neutral, I'll go into a Freaky Cleaning Frenzy, performing piddly tasks that don't matter a whit and will never be noticed.

For no reason I'd attempt to explain, I feel *compelled* to clean out the walk-in entry closet which we haven't been able to walk *into* for months. Although a two-hour keelhaul results in the disposal of tons of accumulated crud, enough remains that nothing short of a search warrant will induce me to open its door to the general public.

Kitchen cabinets get straightened, as does the refrigerator's interior, even though I really wouldn't care to associate with anyone nosy enough to check whether my veggie cans are rowed by species, or who gives a hoot what foodstuffs are currently fossilizing inside the fridge.

Under the influence of a Freaky Cleaning Frenzy, watering nearly terminal houseplants and snipping off a few thousand dead leaves become a priority. If I'm seriously crazed, repotting all those tightly wadded root balls is perceived as no less than a crisis-intervention procedure.

Lemon oiling woodwork, baseboards, and furniture feet comes next, even though neither will be noticed unless a guest pops out a contact lens and starts crawling around the room on all fours. But that possibility is enough to send the dust rag down the "wall" sides of everything we own.

And the more projects I complete, the more I'll find that, under the influence of a Freaky Cleaning binge:

• Straightening the stuff routinely dumped on dresser tops leads to straightening the contents of the drawers.

• Wiping down the miniblinds advances rapidly to spritzing the haze off the windows they're supposed to hide. An outside temperature smaller than my shoe size is all that will prevent me from hosing last season's insect remains off the screens.

• Taking a swipe at the stove's handles and knobs evolves into spraying a thick layer of de-gunker in the oven, which leads to dunking all the burner pans in the sink for a soak, restacking all the cookie sheets and muffin tins rattling in the bin below, and sticking the exhaust fan's filter in the dishwasher.

• Simple sofa-pillow plumping becomes a flipping over of the cushions, which necessitates removing loose change, stray socks, candy wrappers, spit-out candy, and yukky used tissues. And more than likely, a smidge of upholstery shampooing.

• Long-held good intentions to divide the contents of two gargantuan eight-by-sixteen-foot bookshelves into fiction and nonfiction, with tomes arranged alphabetically by author and

spine-height, is an "around to it" whose time has suddenly come.

Then, an hour before guests arrive, as if picnicking on the linoleum was planned, the kitchen floor *must* be rendered eat-off-it clean. That a coat of even the fastest-drying wax won't dry in time doesn't matter as long as a shine's left behind.

With only minutes remaining to get the hostess looking the mostest, even though she's now too tired to care in the leastest, I'll catch my still-wet-from-the-shower self trying to dress for the evening while compulsively aligning every pair of shoes in my closet so their toes point due south.

Granted, these Freaky Cleaning sessions do get the house in order. No small sense of accomplishment comes from knowing that in only one day, a Humble Hovel can be transformed into a Comely Castle like those depicted in the magazines fanned with geometric precision on the coffee table.

But I finally realized that special nights with friends à la the old Löwenbräu commercials rarely included a shot of the hostess nodding off in the nachos.

And besides struggling to be sociable in spite of a post-scrubathon stupor, it's depressingly evident that housework, whether it's done daily or in a preguest frenzy, is too much like a Mideast peace agreement: the results don't last very long.

Rather than let these uncontrollable frenzies leave me forever too pooped to party, the next time a get-together is on the calendar, I've promised myself to hardly lift a finger beforehand.

Specifically, only the left index one, to reserve a table for four, nonsmoking section, please.

There's No Pool Like a New Pool

My children's breakfast-table countdowns tracking how many days of the school year remained reminded me that the season for chaperoning them to the swimming pool was nigh.

Although maternal pool duty is kind of fun at the outset, after several weeks of having my posterior pinched between lounge chair straps, swatting sweat bees, and faithfully applauding a Son or Daughter's 1,746,941st underwater handstand, I'll admit, the thrill is pretty much gone.

And in my case, being a pool mom is stressful. Whereas my peers have the freedom to relax behind a rip-roarin' romance novel or stretch out on the tummy to even their tan, I must stay ever vigilant.

Regardless of enormous investments in private swimming lessons, my children simply *cannot* get the hang of the Dead Man's Float, much less flail butterfly-style across the pool.

This deficiency doesn't bother them, but since it's difficult for me to distinguish between Child-Who's-Sinking-Like-a-Rock-and-Potentially-Drowning and Child-Who's-Sinking-

Like-a-Rock-Because-It's-One-of-Her-Best-Things, my adrenaline level stays at full alert.

Then, an advertising circular inspired a compromise to this dilemma: according to the ad, buying an aboveground pool for the backyard would provide water enough for fun and frolicking, but it had no "deep end" to lure the flotationally impaired into certain peril.

Plus, patronizing the backyard swimmers' snack bar—commonly known as the kitchen—would save me a fortune on pool-side soft drinks, candy bars, and chips. And, I figured, some measure of lifeguard duty could be done while gazing out the windows of my air-conditioned, sweat-bee-free living room.

I chose the Jumbo Seasider model primarily because the photo on the front of the box portrayed a veritable *herd* of splashing, happy youngsters batting beach balls and riding various species of inflated amphibians.

Unfortunately, due to its "X-tra-Hi-Grade, Puncture-Pruf, Heavy-Duty Liner" Jumbo's shipping carton weighed approximately as much as a queen-sized sleeper sofa. But with offspring pushing from the inside of the station wagon and me pulling on the other end, the box finally flumed out the tailgate like a rectangular torpedo.

As luck would have it, we immediately decided that its landing site was also its best construction site, mostly because (a) we didn't have a crane handy to move Jumbo elsewhere, and (b) the grass was already dead there, anyhow.

While the package's boldly printed E-Z TO ASSEMBLE promise further indicated that no one employed by the Jumbo Seaside Pool Company could spell worth a lick, for once, that statement seemed to have some truth to it.

After forming a humongous circle with the stiff, corrugated plastic side walls, all I had to do was nut-and-bolt the ends

41

together. Centering the liner within the sidewall's circle leaving an overhanging, three-inch lip was simpler than I anticipated, too.

Several cuticles were sacrificed sliding the snap trim over the lapped liner and top edge of the sidewall, but to my delight, Jumbo was ready to fill in record time.

Only I'll never understand how accidentally spilling a cup of water on the kitchen floor causes a miniature lake to form on the linoleum, yet intentional floods à la a garden hose take darn near forever.

Hours later, when Jumbo was about half-full, I noticed it was developing a serious starboard slant. Thinking a tug on the liner would remedy the problem, I bent over, grabbed double handfuls of "X-tra-Hi-Grade" plastic, and *jerked* . . . which instantly set off a monstrous tidal wave—which unhinged a section of the snap trim—which unlapped a section of the liner—which made the sidewall buckle ominously outward.

It was readily apparent that the buckled section could be eased back into its circular configuration if a couple of hundred gallons of water would only *cooperate* and stay at the far side of the pool for a few minutes.

As it was, whenever I attempted to straighten the side a fraction, the buckle got bigger, thereby unhinging another foot or so of snap trim—*and* the liner it was supposed to secure.

Naturally, the water level was now rising with a speed not seen since Noah, and letting go of the liner long enough to turn the faucet off would likely irrigate the yard to rice patty proportions.

After the kids scoured the neighborhood for every able-bodied, nonnapping playmate, I assigned each child a section of liner to hold while I zipped the lip securely under the trim.

Although this process looked pretty much like a game of Drop the Handkerchief, with me permanently "It," our "E-Z to Assemble" (but incredibly difficult to fill) Jumbo Seasider was officially open for business.

Not only are the kids enjoying the luxury of their own private pool, complete with free-for-the-asking snacks, I've reaped an unexpected benefit myself.

I'd heard for years that swimming is among the best aerobic exercises, and by golly, there's no doubt that I'm shaping up with every lap I do around ours.

So what if they're done at approximately fifteen-minute intervals around the *outside* of the pool, while resnapping good 'ol Jumbo's forever floppy liner?

On a daily basis, I'll bet I'm doing as many laps as an Olympic contender, but *I* don't even have to get my hair wet.

Good *Mothers* Do

f there's one facet of Motherhood I should have known better than to even *try*, it's Girl Scout troop leadership. My tenure as an actual Girl Scout was certainly proof-positive that I'm profoundly craft-impaired, and that I am *not* of the camping-is-fun persuasion.

Except during a troop organizational meeting, the district coordinator's impassioned plea for a volunteer leader was fraught with "*good* mothers *do*" implications, and morally suasive hints that lacking such wholesome, Scout-like experiences, our daughters were likely destined to become biker chicks or rock star groupies.

As a result, I turned a deaf ear to the intelligent side of my brain, which was screaming, "Are you *nuts?*" and leaped at the chance to become Troop 19's fearless leader.

No war hero or Super Bowl–winning football team has ever received accolades comparable to those heaped on me before the ink on the sign-up sheet was dry. Only later did I figure out that those other moms' tears of gratitude were actually sobs of relief.

At the first meeting, I realized any one of my beanied third-graders was infinitely more capable of stitching together a "sit upon" than I was. Since I've long believed that delegation is key to good management, I promoted Becky, my most needle-adept trooper, to the never-before-heard-of office of Crafts Captain.

Becky's enviable glitter, tongue depressor, poster paint, and loop-looming abilities freed me for adult leadership roles such as taking attendance, distributing snacks, monitoring the rest room, scrubbing glue off the tabletops, and pretty much just showing up for the meetings and acting leaderlike. Other than Missy Janklow's getting our troop's Christmas float disqualified from competition by mooning her little brother (even though she *swore*, Scouts' honor, that he mooned her *first*) all our meetings and day field trips went as smoothly as clockwork—until Cookie Month reared its ugly head.

At the outset, charging my troops with jotting advance orders for as many boxes as they (and their parents) could sell, then delivering the goodies and collecting the loot, seemed relatively simple. As it should have been.

But no one warned me that multiple case lots of everything from chocolate mints to Savannahs would, upon delivery in a truck large enough to transport Mrs. Jumbo *and* Dumbo, alter my living room's decor from Early Parenthood to Early Warehouse.

Or that regional headquarters would add a few dozen extra cases to our presold shipment, ostensibly as incentive for additional sales, which are pretty difficult to come by when several thousand equally overstocked Scouts are likewise peddling them all over town.

Nor could I have predicted that on delivery day, half my troopers would succumb to the flu, chicken pox, or a rampant loss of ambition. Or that an unprecedented number of preorders were made to renters who'd moved, relatives who'd died, and home-alone latchkeyers whose parents decided to "teach him (or her) a lesson" by refusing delivery.

About the time I was seriously considering torching the remaining stock and filing a "spontaneous combustion" claim on our homeowner's insurance, my troopers' parents generously purchased the leftovers, just as I presume parents have since some high-ranking, childless, national Girl Scout organization board member got the bright idea, "Hey, let's have the kids sell cookies every year as a fund-raising project!"

No sooner was that snafu settled than it was time for the end-of-the-school-year overnight at Camp Tuzigoot. Supposedly, its Indian name meant "crooked water" after the camp's meandering creek. Other leaders swore "Tuzigoot" actually translated as "disgusting, mosquito-tick-and-chigger-infested swampland."

Historically, loading the car and unloading the car were the full extent of my camping capabilities, although I invariably got stuck with latrine duty during my long-ago stint as a Scout. Naturally, this is about the only camp chore for which no badge is awarded.

Perhaps that lack of a colorful, embroidered outhouse-depicting medallion to proudly affix on my Official Scout Badge Sash permanently affected my attitude, but I've never understood why people willingly spend *hundreds* of dollars on camping equipment, then drive *hundreds* of miles into the wilderness to sleep on rocks, pee in coffee cans, and dine on food charred to briquette consistency, which, if served to them at home, would be deemed too digusting to feed Fido.

Yet, there must be a special place reserved in heaven for any mother/Girl Scout leader who escorts a dozen eight-year-olds into the forest primeval—and survives. Or at least, there darn sure *better* be.

Before the Big Day, because I owned none of the recommended equipment beyond "pillow, bath towel, facecloth," a trip to the army surplus store was in order.

Once I'd checked off all the items on my list, the preponderance of camouflagic, plug-ugly green gear made me appear to be launching a one-woman commando raid. I'd even splurged and bought a camo-print sleeping bag, marked down to an incredible $7.95—a small price to pay not to drag my own sheets and blankets into the bug-infested boondocks.

Bright and early the next Saturday morning, we were en route to Camp Tuzigoot. Since none of us could remember the words to "Kookaburra," the troopers sang numerous choruses of "Ninety-Nine Bottles of Beer on the Wall."

Upon our arrival, despite the definite aura of a combination Red Cross Disaster Site and Tornado Aftermath, I was confident that my girls and I had the stamina, courage, and determination to last the required twenty-four hours.

Humming the refrain to Helen Reddy's "I Am Woman," I divided the crew into squads of four and assigned each a tent. Because this overnight presented a major badge-earning opportunity, most of the chores, including gathering wood for the campfire, collecting weenie-roasting/marshmallow-toasting sticks, and generally policing the area, were the kids' forte.

While they got their rosters in gear, I lugged my stuff to the Leader's Tent. In the manner of rank having privilege, this canvas edifice was staked nearest the latrine. As long as the wind stayed its current south-southwesterly course, that could be considered a plus.

Tying back the flap, mine eyes beheld incontrovertible evidence that every varmint within a hundred-mile radius had whiled away the winter months munching on my cot's mattress and pooping in my tent. Innumerable shredded tufts of cotton batting vied for floor space with the world's largest repository of rodent dooties, creating nature's definition of a toxic waste dump.

Though a shovel would have been more appropriate, I broomed out my quarters, environmentally consciously depositing all aforementioned deposits in an empty box which I would immolate to ashes after the night's campfire ceremonies were completed.

With my tent as clean as a snaggled, twenty-straw broom could get it and my gear stashed neatly away, it was time to start the campfire.

In their exuberance, the girls had piled up enough tinder, kindling, and logs to roast an entire buffalo herd, but its height did obscure me from view as I squirted the pyre with a couple of quarts of charcoal starter.

So *what* if that petroleum product wasn't exactly mentioned as de rigueur in the *Leader's Handbook*? I knew my own limitations, including no *earthly* desire to spend hours huffing and puffing at teensy little embers trying to coax them into actual flames—and failing, miserably.

When I tossed a match on the heap, the resulting w-h-o-o-s-h instantly remedied any near-future need to pluck my eyebrows. However, the blaze nicely warmed the chilling night air, and the girls were astounded to find that an inferno could cook weenies faster than a microwave. That marshmallows toasted to a beveragelike consistency in mere nanoseconds meant that, probably for the first time in scouting history, the supply of s'mores outstripped the demand.

A lovely medley of traditional campfire songs sung well back from the fire followed, along with the traditional reading of the founding mother Juliette Lowe's life story, finale-ed by the traditional campfire-told tale starring a wandering, one-handed psychopath. The latter certainly enhanced the goggle-eyed listeners' need to visit the latrine before bedding down for the night.

I patrolled the perimeter by flashlight a few times, issuing the same well-remembered leader-style threats I'd heard and hadn't obeyed either when I was a child.

Since the campfire was safely under control but still potent enough to discourage roving wolf packs, bears, or other potential predators, I hied to my own tent to read a while by flashlight beam—something I hadn't done for more years than I cared to calculate.

Because the temperature had dropped to unseasonably small digits, I removed only my grimy sneakers, figuring I could wriggle out of my jeans later while warmly esconced inside my new, bargain-priced sleeping bag.

Except when I inserted my lower extremities, a goodly amount of my upper extremities remained unbagged. Thinking my feet hadn't really touched bottom, I sharply tugged the top, which immediately buckled my knees to approximately my earlobes.

This position did bring my camo cocoon to my shoulders, yet I seriously questioned whether I could sleep in a position similar to that adopted for routine gynecological examinations.

Undoubtedly, I was the proud owner of a piece of camping equipment designed for one of Snow White's seven roommates. And because of the Siberian Express gusting through my tent's flaps, I decided it was my destiny to become the eighth, known in perpetuity (and posthumously) as Freezy.

I did, somehow, manage to drift off, but then too many cups of Kool-Aid coupled with uncontrollable shivering put my bladder into overdrive about every hour on the hour. In blatant defiance of regulations requiring a hike to yonder's rickety relief station, I got no farther than the back outside corner of my tent and gave not even the slightest *rip* whether I was breaking any rules or *not*.

Rising with the sun revealed the entire campsite blanketed in glittering frost—a lovely sight, but hardly a welcome one to my teeth-chattering, starving troops or to me, as I'd just suffered twelve hours of borderline hypothermia.

The fire was out, and without any charcoal starter remaining, nothing short of a flamethrower was going to get it started again. This put a serious crimp in the breakfast menu of canned-biscuit-dough doughnuts to be deep fried in a dutch oven set atop the fire's rock border, and a vat of hot chocolate to be heated likewise.

What's a fearless leader to do under the circumstances? Why, act as if I'd planned that unfortunate turn of events on purpose to test my troopers' mettle, of course. And they certainly came through in the clinch.

In no time, Becky the Crafts Captain was passing her beanie to collect money none of the girls were supposed to have brought on the trip, squad leaders were barking orders to break camp, and their underlings were tossing stuff in the van as if bailing a boat in reverse.

Once precautionary buckets of water were sloshed on the former campfire, the trash was bagged and loaded, and a head count taken, it was full speed ahead back to civilization and our unanimously approved destination.

At the next meeting, I distributed various badges rewarding the numerous camping skills the girls' acquired, plus badges acknowledging their teamwork and helpfulness.

But I think they were proudest of the emblem I had specially made to honor their hunger-relieving ingenuity. And I couldn't imagine anything that would better signify such Supreme Savvy Campership than a crimson circlet emblazoned with a pair of golden arches.

Them and Theirs

Never keep up with the Joneses.

Drag them down to your level.

QUENTIN CRISP

Babs the Pool Babe

Now that I'm all grown up—not to mention out—my views on spending the summer poolside have changed. Personally, I'd rather scrub toilet bowls than make a swimsuit statement by exposing almost as much personhood as I did on my honeymoon.

If all those magazine articles entitled "Swimsuits That Hide Your Figure Flaws" were believable, most of my blah body image would be curable. Except photographs of lithe, absolutely flawless-figured nymphs posed in those "miracle" swimsuits do make me question the veracity of that concept.

How well I remember when Younger Son was not old enough to frequent our neighborhood pool without adult supervision. His three older siblings did meet the age requirement for attending a minor, but it seemed there was nothing like a little brother who "acts like a total doofus" to put a crimp in their budding summer romances. In no uncertain terms, the Big Three made it clear that they'd rather the general public remained unaware that said doofus was related to them.

Realizing that to them the realm of responsible chaperonage would be limited to (a) waiting until Brother's third sinking before considering a rescue or (b) casually identifying the body after the fact, I got designated as the official tagalong, by default.

With saddlebags protruding and my torso bound so tightly in spandex that I could hardly breathe, Son and I trudged off to the pool together. And with every step, I vowed that if he didn't thank me someday for such a selfless sacrifice designed to aid and abet myriad happy childhood memories, I'd cut him out of the will.

Naturally, since my self-esteem was already about three quarts low, the first person I saw was my neighbor, Babs, lounging on a chaise like a sleek, coconut-oiled, tawny Siamese. At forty-five, this woman is living proof that some of us have some of it, most of us don't have any of it, and a smidgen of shes have it *all*.

That her bikini top is four sizes larger than the bottom—the exact opposite of most of the adult female population—is instantly, and disgustingly, evident. So is the fact that although she's borne three children, with twins at the get-go, there's nary a stretch mark on her to show for it.

Rumor has it that jaunts to the mailbox are enough to tan Babs the same shade as wheat toast, whereas I could braise on my deck for days and stay as white as Wonder bread.

And she not only actually *swims*, her palomino pageboy looks as lovely sopping wet as it does following a casual finger combing and breeze dry.

Like a true masochist, I couldn't take my eyes off this sin against nature. I watched as Babs showed off her graceful swan dive, then twirled a couple of full gainers off the board. However, following these mermaidlike maneuvers, she didn't emerge from the water looking like a human raccoon. *Her* waterproof mascara really *was*.

Of course, all that exercise can sure make a gal hungry, so Babs strutted daintily to the snack bar for a double cheeseburger deluxe, jumbo Snickers, and a bag of barbecue potato chips.

On the return trip, she saw me drooling enviously at her munchables, which *I* couldn't have treated myself to even if I'd just plowed the north forty behind a mule.

Probably without malice and undoubtedly without forethought, in her sultry, southern drawl she explained, "Ah jes' *try* and *try* to put some meat on these little 'ol bones, but ah cain't seem to gain an *ow-unce*."

Poor ba-by. I couldn't help wondering whether she thought cellulite was the stuff that makes grass green.

Okay, so Babs is basically a decent person—quickly fills in when a baby-sitter craps out, promptly returns stuff she borrows, and volunteers to pick up the mail, newspapers, water the plants, and feed Fido for vacationing neighbors.

In fact, if she just looked a little more like Granny Clampett and a lot less like Elly May, we'd probably be good friends.

But until Babs the Pool Babe's thighs generate static electricity when she walks, her underarm flab waves one direction while her hand goes the other, and there're red, razor-bladed racing stripes zipping up both shins, we're a tad shy of common ground to build a relationship on.

Oh, sure, we could talk about our kids—except hers excel at everything, and my four mostly excel at breathing.

Husbands are usually the second favorite subject for female discussion, and while mine gives me numerous causes for complaint, her six-foot-two-and-studly spouse reportedly does *all* the cooking and grocery shopping, *always* puts his dirty clothes in the hamper *and* washes, dries, and irons them—*and*, presumably, leaps tall buildings in a single bound.

That they live in a dream house, and drive matching convertible sports cars should come as no surprise. And clothes? I've yet to see Babs in the same outfit twice.

It was depressing enough to have Mattel's two perfect specimens thrust upon me as role models during my childhood. But darned if I'll ever know what 1 did to deserve living right next door to Babs, and that living doll she's married to . . . Ken.

Buying Shoppers vs. Shopping Shoppers

*A*nn, my best buddette, recently flew in for a visit. I anticipated her arrival with enormous enthusiasm—and just the teensiest dash of dread.

After donning baggy sweats, we bared our faces, then our souls with nonstop, slumber-party-style schmoozing fueled by friendship, adult beverages, and junk food chomped right out of their boxes and bags.

That we *need* these biannual, high-calorie, jabbering jamborees is something guys don't get, and long-distance *amigas* don't get enough of.

But amid our purposely unscheduled calendar of events, we made an obligatory trek to the mall—borderline bliss for Ann, whose home is forty-five minutes from anything remotely retail oriented and eight hundred miles from me, i.e., someone to go shopping *with*.

Except despite the numerous common bonds that tie us, I'd rather watch mildew grow on a shower curtain than shop—a character flaw Ann's determined to correct. Much like scotch or caviar, she figures that with regular imbibing, I'll eventually develop a taste for fondling and "oooh/ahhing" over about eighty-seven million dollars' worth of stuff I have no intention of buying.

But I've never been one who shops just to *shop*. I'm a buyer-shopper: I shop for things I need, purchase them as quickly as possible, and go home. Even as a teenager when Saturdays and shopping were synonymous, those on-the-town afternoons were *not* merely opportunities for Recreational Loitering. They had a *purpose*. Primarily, trolling for guys.

Ann, however, approaches shopping with the fervor of King Arthur's searching for the Holy Grail. Yet while Arthur did dawdle across most of Great Britain, at least he knew what he was looking *for*. Most of the time, Ann's "just looking," and fondling and gasping, over every shred of merchandise in every store in the entire mall—which only *seems* as big as England.

This merchandising monolith is approximately the same size as the downtown shopping district it bankrupted. Its site is in the suburbs (*meaning:* a former cow pasture), allowing plenty of room for expansion (*meaning:* lots for lots of fast food franchises are available at grossly inflated prices).

What to call this suburban sprawl undoubtedly involved *weeks* of intense brainstorming before the traditional tack was taken: naming it after the species of trees that got bulldozed into mulch during construction. Fancier moniker notwithstanding, everyone refers to it as simply The Mall, which it probably should have been named in the first place, but none ever are.

Presumably, mall developers are also graduates of the Don't-Know-a-Hill-from-a-Hole-in-the-Ground School of Architecture. Like countless others nationwide, the local super-shop-a-rama is centered on a sunken plat, surrounded by a tilty parking lot approximately as big as the Ponderosa.

Not only do I always expect to see Ben Cartwright and the boys herding cars over that vast, asphalted acreage, but as a result of the building's bottom-of-a-bowl positioning, a wide, curb-high moat is formed around The Mall's entire circumference by rainwater, snow melt, and deluges from continual charity car washes.

Like deer fording a stream, Ann and I had to leap this permanent puddle to gain access to the "climate-controlled" Magic Kingdom of Commerce. Only the climate within mostly ranges from a Sahara-like scorch during winter months to Siberian chilblains in the summer. Between such extremes, the complex's crack maintenance team keeps the thermostat pegged at "stuffy."

For a buyer-shopper like me, such elongated emporia mean the odds of the two stores I plan to patronize being located within the same area code are roughly zilch.

This is why food courts are as common in malls as hordes of exceptionally hearty walkers hup-twoing at a pace usually reserved for evading packs of large dogs. Besides the main thoroughfare's smattering of wobbly benches shoved against the trunks of towering and decidedly carnivorous-looking potted plants, these "patio areas" are the only place the weary can take a load off their loafers.

But women in particular are incapable of parking their posteriors at snack tables without buying "some little something" to sort-of pay for the privilege. Because even a soft drink Table Toll costs a dollar or more, this quirk can be counted on to boost the food vendors' bottom lines.

Ann circumvented that park-'n'-pay tendency with ease: Like the TV battery bunny, she kept going, and going, and going, until her internal radar honed in on an item demanding closer scrutiny. Without announcing her intentions, she veered off into a store, leaving me, much to the annoyance of numerous passersby, obliviously babbling to myself.

When I found her, she was deeply engrossed in a ritual that truly separates the shopping-shoppers from the buying-shoppers. With her expression as serious as a practicing neurosurgeon, she was microscopically examining a blouse, twisting it to and fro, and rubbing the material between her fingers.

Emitting a chorus of deeply thoughtful "Hmmms," she repeatedly perused it from an arm's length away, then up close, and back again, as if reeling in a trophy trout, before mournfully declaring that if *only* it were longer/shorter, fuller/more tapered, a different color, long sleeved/short sleeved, of a heavier/lighter/plainer/patterned fabric—pretty much anything other than what it actually *was*—it would be simply "darling."

Yet Ann continued gazing at it rapturously as if expecting the Garment Fairy to fly by and make the item magically metamorphose before her very eyes. When *that* didn't happen, she pawed through the entire rack she'd pawed through *twice* already just in case she had missed a model meeting her specifications.

By the time she'd fully reconnoitered Ladies' Ready to Wear, I'd scouted sixteen departments on four floors, bought a pair of shoes, a handful of greeting cards, checked out an advertised white sale, purchased a dress shirt required for Son's school play, and been squirted twice by the Cosmetics Department Sniper, who makes her living gassing innocent customers with an atomizer containing an extremely expensive and perfectly *noxious* perfume.

Yet Ann's shopper-shopping siege didn't really begin until lust for a new skirt overcame her. Automatically, my eyes rolled heavenward, even though she promised mere seconds would elapse between "May I help you ladies?" and "Will that be cash or charge?"

To my surprise, Ann *did* grab a couple of "possibles" in record time and sprinted away for a try-on. I'd have been heartened by her uncustomary quickness had she ever shown any Houdini-of-the-Dressing-Room tendencies.

Before I'd finished counting *every* leaf in the carpet's motif, she emerged, attired in a black skirt, and started pirouetting in front of the trifold mirror.

"What do you think?" she asked.

"It looks fine—"

"What do you mean 'fine'? You mean okay fine? or terrific fine? or just so-so fine?"

"It looks *fine* fine. Really."

"You don't like it, do you?"

"I *said* it looks FINE, *okay?*"

With that, she huffed back to the cubicle, returning a quarter hour later in a gray version.

"I think I like this one better, don't you?" she inquired rhetorically.

Having learned my lesson, I replied, "That one does fit a bit nicer."

"Uh-huh—so you *didn't* like the black skirt after all, did you?"

"I liked it *fine!* I just like this one better, all right?"

"Well, *I* like the black one better."

"Then buy the black one."

"Its belt is more versatile, and it was the perfect length. Don't you think?"

"Absolutely. Buy it."

With a thumbnail wedged between her incisors, she hedged, "Oh gosh, I don't know. C'mon, help me decide. Why didn't you like the black one?"

"I don't know . . . I just didn't."

"A-*ha! First* you said it looked *fine,* and now you *admit* you didn't like it. I'll bet you don't *really* like *this* one, either."

Good taste precludes relating my reply verbatim, but in essence, it suggested where Ann could put both skirts without risk of sun fading.

"I'll show *you,*" she snipped, before stomping back to the dressing room. "I'm gonna buy *both* of them! How do you like *that!*"

Temporarily, I did identify and sympathize with men who have no clue how to decipher the inner workings of female minds—until I realized that Ann's nonsensical modus operandi was akin to a man who painstakingly wraps a leaky kitchen faucet with three hundred and fifty-one yards of electrical tape rather than simply replace its worn washer.

Not until Ann accumulated enough stuff to have foundered our Westward Ho-ing foreparents' wagons did she answer my whines to go home in the affirmative. Immediately, I was reminded *why* she considers my companionship on such shopping excursions so critical: because pack mules aren't allowed inside The Mall's confines.

While our fingers were slowly being severed by God-only-knew-how-many shopping bag handles, we shuffled out The Mall's main entrance only to be confronted by the lot's innumerable rows, containing about a jillion cars each. The majority of these vehicles were the exact color and make as mine, but on closer inspection never were.

No, *my* car was virtually *miles* farther from the door than it had seemed when I parked it next to a "landmark" light pole—not realizing the lot featured at least three dozen identical light poles, all of which now had red coupes, just like mine, skootched beside their bases.

That thirty-five other bag-lugging, red-car-owning Bedouins would also have to wander hither and yon for precisely the same reason lent some measure of comfort.

For all the frustration this buyer-shopper suffers in the company of Ann, an Olympic gold medal–caliber shopper-shopper, other acquaintances have questioned why I don't just drop her off at the door to do her most beloved "thing," then pick her up at a predetermined time, such as noonish the following Tuesday.

To those folks, I say that for all my complaining, best friendship is just as Eustace Budgell defined it: "a strong and habitual inclination in two persons to promote the good and happiness of one another."

Ann certainly keeps up her end of the bargain by *always* exclaiming, the instant she rushes through the airport arrival gate and hugs me breathless, "Jeez Louise, you're as skinny as a teenager—and you look more like one every time I see you!"

No untruer words are ever spoken but by a loving, forever friend.

Who I'd follow anywhere.

Even to The *#&$^% *Mall*.

Aesop's Automobile

*I*f I had my way, whoever invented the car alarm would be put before a firing squad. And after being kept awake for seventy-two consecutive hours by assorted sirens, buzzers, bells, and horns, there's no chance that any of the shooters' rifles would be loaded with blanks.

Granted, I live in an area where teenagers in a Saturday-night street-sign-swiping frenzy constitutes a major crime wave. But I don't believe such devices are effective even in major metropolitan areas.

My introduction to, and immediate dislike of, burglar beepers began the day a neighbor drove home a spiffy new Pontiac. Since even a midrange vehicle's sticker price now equals what a three-bedroom, two-bath, ranch-style home cost in 1969, the coupe's built-in theft protector seemed like an appropriate watchdog to protect the owner's investment.

Problem was, it became immediately apparent that anything from a prowling pussycat to a cloud passing in front of the moon set the siren to wailing like a banshee. After several consecutive nights of being awakened repeatedly by what constituted a Borealis blue, two-door, snooze alarm, I'd have *applauded* any criminal's attempt to steal it.

Like Aesop's fable about the boy who cried "Wolf!" so often that no one believed him when an actual Big Bad was snapping at his heels, the *last* thing I thought when I heard that oft-*arrooooed* howl was that someone was committing grand theft: auto.

The first things I thought, while putting a pillow over my ears to drown out the dronings, were primarily profanities questioning Neighbor's legitimacy. Next, I pondered why any reasonably intelligent human being would put himself in the position of responding to a hunk of metal's middle-of-the-night cries just as one would a hungry infant's.

As Neighbor's Wife espoused, whenever the car started caterwauling, her spouse bolted from beneath the bedcovers and started patting down the nightstand, searching for the alarm's remote control. Then, with the device in hand, after clipping the door facing with an elbow or stubbing a toe on the banister, he'd totter downstairs and the length of their house continually pushing the gizmo's "reset" button even though he knew he wasn't in range until he was halfway across the kitchen.

Once the siren had been silenced (and Neighbor's Wife divulged that *he* no longer peered out a window for signs of a vehicular vandal's assault, either), Neighbor shuffled back to bed knowing full well that the next moth that used his car's hood for a landing strip would start the alarm, and the entire turning-off process, all over again.

So why didn't he simply disconnect the system and be done with it? When I posed this question to Neighbor, he replied groggily that because he'd shelled out several hundred extra dollars *for* it, he was darn sure going to get his money's worth *from* it.

To my mind, that's logic on a par with driving seventy-five miles to a supermarket grand opening featuring ground chuck at a dollar a pound—then only buying a couple of bucks' worth because you're trying to cut back on the grocery bill.

Judging by a decidedly unscientific poll I just completed, I'd say that it's rare when a wailing car alarm sets any passers-bys' ears on Full Alert. Oh, they'll *hear* it, but considering the frequency of false alarms most folks have been exposed to, they too will more likely cuss the contraption than lend any credence to it.

Case in point: Last week I was walking across a mall's parking lot when an auto alarm started bleating like a crazed billy goat. I traced the racket to a snazzy conversion van two rows ahead and to my right. Not only was the vehicle emitting its electronic coyote love call, the head- and taillights were strobing so rhythmically the van seemed as ready for takeoff as a launch-padded space shuttle.

A dozen or more other shoppers glanced in its direction, snickered, then went on about their business. Nary a one was poised to institute a citizen's arrest upon the perpetrator—mostly because there was no one within fifty yards of the berserkmobile to begin with.

While it's true that today's wheels cost a heck of a lot of money, and that both car stripping and car swiping are on the upswing, I don't think on-board alarm systems are the answer.

They're simply too persnickety to be believed, and besides, how's an innocent bystander supposed to determine whether the sheepish-looking fella standing next to the shrieking vehicle is its embarrassed owner or a bandito with larceny in his heart and a lock punch in his pocket?

If it's ever economically feasible for me to buy a brand-new set of gee-whizzy wheels and I catch myself worrying about carjacking, I'll install a much quieter, more dependable, and more effective car-protection device.

The way I figure it, if having a hundred-and-fifty-pound German shepherd in the backseat won't take a bite out of crime, *nothing* will.

Howboutta Holidays

*d*espite their advancing age, my children still spend days compiling helpful, nine-page "wish" lists complete with prices, catalog item numbers, toll-free ordering information, and estimated shipping and handling charges. But it wouldn't be Christmas without that brain racking that comes from having several don't-have-a-clue-what-to-get gift-buying challenges on my holiday shopping list.

These problem people include loved ones who, when asked what they'd like to find under the tree, answer with phrases like, "Oh, you don't have to get me anything," or, "Gosh, I don't know . . . surprise me."

Since such replies are on a par with a restaurant hostess asking the only pair of people in the vestibule, "Table for two?" desperate yet spirited rounds of an ever-popular game called "Howboutta" commence thusly:

> *"Howboutta new bathrobe," I'll inquire to start things off.*
> *"Haven't worn the one you got me last year, yet."*
> *"Okay, howboutta toaster?"*

"Nothing wrong with the old one."

"Howboutta magazine subscription? Reader's Digest or The Saturday Evening Post?"

"Nah. I don't have time to read anymore."

Depending upon the skill levels of the participants, this line of inquiry can continue almost indefinitely, but will eventually conclude with the answerer repeating either, "You don't have to get me anything," or, "Gosh, I don't know . . . surprise me."

By the time I've elbowed my way through numerous department stores, discount stores, hardware stores, book stores, one-of-a-kind boutiques, and every emporium in between hoping for an inspiration (or a reasonably priced facsimile thereof), the temptation to *really* surprise those folks by *not* getting them anything is nigh overwhelming.

After lengthy telephone consultations with similarly stumped friends because (a) misery loves company and (b) two heads are supposedly better than one, I usually end up buying all nonhinters whatever weird, battery-operated doohickey the Ronco Corporation or Popeil Industries have been advertising every day on television, at approximately three-minute intervals, since Halloween.

While this strategy takes care of the chronically clueless, other gift gauntlets that must be run before my credit cards max out—or I do—include:

• Quests for mailable merchandise that will actually fit in the empty boxes that have been crammed in a closet for an entire year expressly for that purpose. These gifts must also be sufficiently nonfragile to arrive at their destinations in the same number of pieces they started out with, but must not be fruitcake because of the inherent risk of, in the manner of swallows returning to Capistrano, the sucker coming back from whence it went, next Christmas.

• A definitely nongeeky and preferably *awesome* fourth-grade gift-exchange item priced at or below the two-dollar limit—including sales tax.

• The name of the absolutely numero uno toy my grand-daughter wants more than anything in the Whole, Wide World, which she whispered in Santa's ear a couple of weeks ago, and now, because of her unshakeable belief that The Big Guy's got her covered, will *not* tell anyone else.

• An apt substitute for a long-promised gift that I put on layaway in October to ensure its availability, then was told when I returned to retrieve it that "somebody must have sold it by accident," and that it is now "out of stock" at that locale and everywhere else on the North American continent.

• "Little somethings" for newspaper routepersons, letter carriers, next-door neighbors, a secretary, boss, or bowling buddy, a favorite baby-sitter, a son's girlfriend, a daughter's boyfriend, the dog, the cat, and a couple of gender-neutral extras to insure against getting caught empty-handed by someone I overlooked.

• A compromise gift for an adolescent who's convinced that both parents have the fashion sense of cocker spaniels, thereby eliminating clothes from the list of potential presents, but *does* consider them capable of choosing and paying for a majorly cool new car equipped with power steering, power brakes, power windows, power locks, power headlights, power seats, and a stereo system which can be heard *thunk-thunk-a-THUNK*ing from two blocks away.

• A present for dear old Uncle Milford who really does have everything—in fact, has two or three of them because he never gets rid of anything, even after it's broken.

Exasperating as all the above may be, these gift-buying challenges are only training exercises for the biggest boondoggle of them all: Tearing to The Mall to Help Your Teenage Son Find a Gift for His Girlfriend Forty-five Minutes Before All the Stores Close on Christmas Eve.

If given the choice, even the most confirmed shopaholic would, at this point in the season, rather scrub grease stains off the garage floor. However, compassion for the poor girl who will likely receive the last Whitman's Sampler on the shelf at the nearest convenience store if such adult supervision is denied, inspires quick, albeit grumpy, cooperation.

En route, a couple of minor details finally rate mention: (a) Son has a grand total of $1.73 jingling in his jeans, and (b) he has illusions of grandeur regarding what he wants to bestow upon his sweetheart, mostly because Mom's been coerced into financing it, too.

Thankfully, there's nothing like the sound of stores' security doors whanging shut in all directions to banish visions of diamond stud earrings and glittery tennis bracelets dancing in Son's head. A department store jewelry counter's nongold, non-gem-encrusted trinket slashed to 50 percent off is jubilantly declared "Perfect!"—as if Mom hadn't made that same observation several minutes earlier.

In the waning wee hours before the annual Christmas Morning Shredathon begins, I'll be struck by the realization that by some miracle, another year's pondering, planning, purchasing, and multitudinous present wrapping is at an end.

I'll rest assured—if not for long—that just as in years past, Santa will get most of the credit for bringing that sleighload of good-girl-and-boy toys and all that Ronco-Popeil paraphernalia glittering beneath the tree.

And then it will, without a doubt, occur to me just as my head hits the pillow, that, just as in years past, *I forgot to get the %$#&^ batteries for 'em!*

The Covey Syndrome

Once upon a time, a car commercial costarred a guy standing atop a crested butte, totally alone but for the four-wheel-drive vehicle that got him there.

While the narrator extolled the virtues of the billy goat–like getawaymobile, the camera panned the vast, peaceful, and completely personless vista surrounding the driver. The sales pitch ended with a shot of a similar-modeled, multicar convoy careening into view, then circling that once-lone stranger like a posse.

I immediately identified with that unfortunate fellow, because I, too, am victimized by what I call the Covey Syndrome.

Due to this unfortunate crowd-attracting ability, I've considered contacting NASA to volunteer my services as a space invader. There's no doubt in my mind that landing me on Mars would result in the planet's immediate overpopulation. Or, I could become a "crowd consultant" for politicians—my mere presence at a campaign rally would draw listeners like a dark sweater draws lint.

A typical week provides any number of follow-the-leader–style qualifications. For example, I intentionally schedule supermarket forays during the store's nonrush hours. This strategy is designed to decrease the possibility of having to arm wrestle a half dozen others for the last package of on-sale toilet paper, nor are serpentine maneuvers à la John Wayne's beachhead landing in *The Sands of Iwo Jima* necessary just to negotiate my buggy down the aisles.

When I arrive at the Sav-A-Mart and park dead-bang in the middle of its deserted, three-acre lot, within seconds, as sure as the sun sets in the west, two other vehicles will whiz into the starboard and port spaces alongside, and a third will ease up on my bow.

Naturally, the coupe claiming the slot on my left will position itself so closely that I'll have to effect a forty-five degree sideways slither to exit my auto and prevent impaling myself with the door handle.

After accumulating everything on my list, plus an additional 522,642 products I didn't know I needed until I saw them on the shelves, I'll saunter toward the fleet of checkout stations.

Since these bunker-shaped counters are buttressed by racks of candy, gum, mints, batteries, magazines, cigarettes, lighters, and palm-sized pamphlets promising the secrets to everything from thin thighs to astrological futures, customers can't see whether there are any actual humans on duty or not. Instead of simply removing all these obstructions, each counter is equipped with a towering, lighted pole to signal whether it's currently operational.

Invariably, whenever I have enough food in my cart to feed the entire state of Rhode Island for a week, the only beacon that'll be beaming is the eight-items-or-less Express Lane's. And because its cashier is so bored she's ghost dancing to

Barry Manilow Muzak, she'll encourage me to come on through.

Although I haven't seen another soul since I passed the produce manager hosing off a crate of rutabagas, about the time half my haul is deposited on the checkout's conveyor belt, nine people will have lined up behind me clutching little more than a head of lettuce, a quart of milk, or a six-pack.

And they won't be glaring at the cashier who *commanded* me to ignore the store's cardinal, eight-or-less rule. No, they're glaring at *me* the same way they would at glops of bubble gum stuck to the soles of their shoes.

I'd dismiss this crowd-attracting trait as further proof that Murphy's Law should be embroidered on my family crest, but it happens so often it defies another of Life's Primary Precepts: the Law of Averages.

Intentionally choosing a central, ten-rows-down seat in a movie theater so sparsely populated that even Nolan Ryan couldn't bean anybody with a Jujube guarantees that before the credits roll, two guys the size of Shaquille O'Neal's bigger brothers will plunk down in the seats in front of me.

Or if meeting a friend at a restaurant for pie, coffee, and conversation, I'll purposely snag booth space in a section totally devoid of other diners. Before the waitperson can deliver ice water and menus, a Walton-family-reunion-sized clan will claim tables within sneezin' distance.

Such Covey Syndrome symptoms are always aggravating, but some can get downright embarrassing.

It never fails that when I'm in need of some personal hygiene products, I'll dawdle around the drugstore perusing its greeting card and cosmetic displays until all other customers, and preferably the cashier, are of the female persuasion. Except the moment I dump an armload of sanitary supplies on the counter, Ms. Cash Register will dash off for a coffee break leaving Sir Stockperson at the helm and three dudes wearing obscenely sloganed, Harley-Davidson T-shirts and smart-alecky smirks will appear out of nowhere.

Call me old-fashioned, but this does not, in my opinion, represent one of womanhood's more stellar moments.

It seems reasonable to assume that living in an area where there are still more cows per square foot than concrete should reap plenty of solitary benefits. However, due to the Covey Syndrome, a lazy day's fishing only stays that way as long as the crappie and bass aren't biting. Once nibbles turn to catches, every "lunker" within a ten-mile radius starts clambering down the riverbank with rod and reel in hand, which turns my quiet commune with nature into a veritable trolling tournament.

Honestly, I'm not antisocial. I've enjoyed meaningful, street-corner conversations with complete strangers while waiting for a traffic light to change. But at those times when I'd prefer remaining poles apart from the general populace, folks gravitate toward me as if I'd just won a mega-million-dollar lottery.

Whether I call it the Covey Syndrome, or better yet, attribute it to a magnetic personality, it's only operational when I want it *least*.

Put me on a back road, in a frog-strangling thunderstorm, with four kids in the car, a flat tire, and a jack buried beneath three tons of peat moss, and sure as the sun sets in the west, *everyone* heads for the hills and *stays* there.

Lefties R Us

During childhood, being a family's lone left-hander means never being allowed to occupy a middle chair at the dinner table. Because a southpaw amidst a row of northpaws screws up the mealtime choreography much like a kangaroo in a conga line, a southwest or northeast corner, slap-upside the corresponding table leg, is declared exclusively Left-winged Territory.

As with most of life's prohibitions, this restriction was considered "no big deal" by everyone except the prohibee.

For some reason, whenever the extended family flocks together, a not-nearly-distant-enough relative seems compelled to remark, "We've never *had* a *southpaw* in the family before," in the same curled-lip tone with which one might say, "We've never *had* a *Two-headed Cyclops* in the family before."

Then, reminiscences of other forebears' oddities ensue, including Great Uncle Archibald's propensity for taking potshots at "spies" who didn't know the day's password, even though studies have shown that lumping left-handedness in the same "oddball" category as ancestral psychoses does nothing to raise a southpaw's self-esteem.

Elementary school is also rife with opportunities for "wrong"-handed discrimination. By about third grade, a lefty's thumb has become permanently creased from using right-handed scissors—not only because the handles are geared for the other-handed, but because the blades are honed that way too, which lends a distinctively "gnawed" appearance to anything cut on a southpawed slant.

That Leonardo da Vinci and Michelangelo—both lefties—became great artists is probably because they expired long before construction paper, snub-nosed scissors, and picky-picky-picky grade-school art teachers were invented.

For the most part, school desks are also designed for righties, which, in combination with continually grinding one's forearm against a notebook's metal spirals, likely contributes to the clawlike "crook" lefty writers are famous for.

To add insult to injury, because of the southpaw's supposed nearer-mine-eyes-to-the-adjacent-right-hander's-paper perspective for cheating, many teachers move the lefties to the far side of the room during tests, though they know darned well the only answers that could possibly be scoped belong to Bruno, the only fifth-grader who shaves.

Southpaws get teased a lot, too: the same classmates who can't for the life of themselves remember that Albany is the capital of New York make much recess hay out of repeating the factoid that Jack the Ripper and the Boston Strangler were left-handed.

Nanny-nanny-boo-booed rebuttals that Benjamin Franklin, Marilyn Monroe, Babe Ruth, and Alexander the Great were, *too*, so *there*, make no impact whatsoever.

With adulthood, left-handedness presents less of a social gaffe, but living in a northpawed world is, at the least, a constant aggravation.

With the exception of the computer and its predecessor, the typewriter—whose left-friendly keyboards are undoubtedly a complete and total accident—machinery of all kinds is geared for the dexterous majority.

From cars to Caterpillar earthmovers, ten-speed bicycles to motorcycles, almost everything with wheels was designed for the convenience of right-handers. That left-handed operators are forced to manipulate said conveyances under less than optimum conditions should give northpaws pause for thought.

If ever in the mood for some Lawn Humor, seek out the nearest neighborhood lefty in the process of starting a pull-cord mower. Trying to zing the string across the engine housing usually results in a spirited man-and-machine fandango, while yanking the cord from the right side, but with the "wrong" hand, will flood the sucker faster than a punk spark plug.

The go gizmos on can openers, microwave ovens, power tools, blow dryers, and curling irons certainly favor right-handers, as do cameras and fishing reels. Believe it or not, even pay phones are guilty of discrimination. With the receiver and its cord invariably tethered on the left, that too-blasted-short, too-blasted-stiff metal-sheathed cable proceeds to practically lynch any southpawed phone customer gamely trying to simultaneously hold said receiver between his right ear and shoulder, reach *over* the dratted cord, and punch in the number, left-handedly.

Another quirk of left-handed life is that most zipper plackets are accessible exclusively from the starboard side. Nor can southpaws sweep left-to-right with a broom because most

have right-to-left-angled straws, or scoop ice cream without leaving knuckle trails in the fudge ripple.

It's also impossible for lefties to bowl, play golf, or baseball without specially made (*read:* more expensive than standard) equipment. But woe still goes to any behind-the-plate positioned, left-handed Little Leaguer—not a single southpaw catcher has ever made it to the Majors.

Considering the innumerable hazards lurking to befall the unwary lefty, is it any wonder they have a reputation for being awkward and accident-prone? Let a northpaw try opening a can of Spam other-handedly, then count the number of fingers remaining afterward. Why, it's more a wonder that lefties have survived at all.

Yet not only are they surviving, they're *thriving:* There was absolutely no doubt that the 1992 presidential election would be won by a southpaw because *all three top contenders* were, as the French call it, "gauche." In fact, four of our last five presidents are gauche: Gerald Ford, Ronald Reagan, George Bush, and Bill Clinton.

Okay, so respectively, one had the grace of a wounded musk ox, one got shot, and the third urped in the Japanese Prime Minister's lap. Recent northpaw presidents haven't been any great shakes either.

Lest the right-winged forget recent history, their side includes a chief executive who couldn't keep either hand to himself, one who cooked the books on a war's progress, another who was not a crook, and an incumbent who couldn't have gotten reelected if he'd run unopposed.

Obviously, which paw one uses to accomplish everyday tasks, be it the forking of food or the signing of presidential proclamations, has absolutely no correlation to competency.

On the other hand (so to speak), it's been scientifically established that the right sphere of the brain controls the left side of the body.

Which means that it's only *lefties* who are in their *right* minds.

And I believe I speak for all proud-to-be southpaws when I say: "Nanny nanny boo boo. So *there*."

If Nobody Sees You Do It, It Doesn't Count

*M*uch like the proverbial trees fall silently in the forest if no one's near to hear them, theoretically some actions don't count against us as long as no one sees them committed.

Life's wonderful ways of cutting we fallible humans some slack now and then include:

IF NOBODY SEES YOU
eat a double-dip hot fudge sundae, the calories don't count.

IF NOBODY SEES YOU
repeatedly Scotch tape a skirt's hem instead of mending it, it doesn't count as laziness.

IF NOBODY SEES YOU
pat down, shake, sniff, or heft your Christmas presents, it doesn't count as peeking.

IF NOBODY SEES YOU
ditch Aisle 2's jar of imported olives amongst Aisle 13's
Post Toasties, it doesn't count as tackiness.

IF NOBODY SEES YOU
ease through a stop-signed intersection out in the boon-
docks, it doesn't count as careless and reckless.

IF NOBODY SEES YOU
accidentally drop a pricey T-bone on the kitchen floor, it
doesn't count as being "dirty."

IF NOBODY SEES YOU
discard one recyclable soda bottle in the regular trash
bin, it doesn't count as environmental abuse.

IF NOBODY SEES YOU
use Spouse's razor to shave your legs, it doesn't count as discourtesy.

IF NOBODY SEES YOU
throw away ketchup, mustard, mayonnaise, or peanut butter containers with smidges left in them, it doesn't count as wastefulness.

IF NOBODY SEES YOU
just *barely* nudge the car parked next to yours with your door, it doesn't count as willful negligence.

IF NOBODY SEES YOU
color your hair, the gray underneath doesn't count as evidence of vanity or aging.

IF NOBODY SEES YOU
weigh yourself, the numbers don't count as being accurate—unless they're smaller than you expected—and you can still knock off a few pounds if you want to.

IF NOBODY SEES YOU
stash a bunch of stuff under the bed, it doesn't count as pack ratting.

IF NOBODY SEES YOU
nod off at your desk, in church, or during your child's school play, it doesn't count as dereliction of duty.

IF NOBODY SEES YOU
wipe your nose on your sleeve because you're out of tissues, it doesn't count as gross.

IF NOBODY SEES YOU
park in a No Parking Zone or Fire Lane for just a few teensy seconds, it doesn't count as civic disobedience.

IF NOBODY SEES YOU
snarf a candy bar, it doesn't count as fattening for adults, and, for children, as spoiling their supper.

IF NOBODY SEES YOU
trip over a sidewalk crack, split the seam of your pants, or blow out a zipper, it doesn't count as embarrassing.

IF NOBODY SEES YOU
drink directly out of a milk jug, juice pitcher, or soda bottle, it doesn't count as disgusting.

IF NOBODY SEES YOU
dump your cooked carrots or Brussels sprouts in the trash, it doesn't count as picky eating.

IF NOBODY SEES YOU
"borrow" Dad's car or bring it back, it doesn't count as grand theft: auto.

IF NOBODY SEES YOU
hide dirty laundry instead of washing it, it doesn't count as slothful.

IF NOBODY SEES YOU
use the last of the toilet paper without spindling a new roll, it doesn't count as inconsiderate.

IF NOBODY SEES YOU
stash the change from writing a grocery check over the amount due, it doesn't count as petty larceny.

IF NOBODY SEES YOU
arrive two hours after curfew, it doesn't count as being late.

IF NOBODY SEE YOU
pinch your little brother, it doesn't count . . . period.

But while pondering all these "see no evil, ain't no evil" proverbials, please keep in mind that:

IF NOBODY SEES YOU SMILE
it doesn't count, either.

My Country

'Tis of Thee

It is by the goodness of God that in our country we have three

unspeakably precious things: freedom of speech, freedom of

conscience, and the prudence never to practice either of them.

MARK TWAIN

Merchandising Motherhood

nce again, I chalked up the goofy Mother's Day gifts I received to Spouse's and Children's decided lack of shopping savvy. It's difficult enough to wax poetic and gracious over a new (and fifth consecutive) electric carving knife at Christmastime, but on my mid-May special day, emitting excited exultations after unwrapping a strawberry-shaped hummingbird feeder is beyond me.

Ditto the reversible, car washing brush/sponge that attaches to the garden hose in such a fashion that it coldly and steadily leaks directly into my tennis shoes.

Or a voluminous, posy-patterned, cotton housecoat that Edith Bunker wouldn't have been caught dead in—but which, with the addition of a couple of stakes and guy wires, she could've *camped* in.

Or the crystal cake plate bestowed upon one who considers uncharred slice 'n' bake cookies a culinary coup.

I guess such snide asides could sound a tad greedy when it's supposed to be the thought that counts. Except I vividly remember the number of times I've searched high and low for a toy one of my children just *had* to have or Life Would No Longer Be Worth Living. And racking my brain for days trying to think of a dazzling gift idea for a spouse who invariably answered my queries regarding what he might want, need, or desire with, "Boy, I could sure use some new *socks*."

It may be self-pity, but after conscientiously meeting or exceeding my family's every gift-receiving expectation, I thought it only fair that I get something sort-of spectacular every millennium or so.

Then, while perusing several Mother's Day sale circulars in the newspaper, I suddenly realized what had been inspiring those frequent faux pas. From department and discount stores to plumbing emporiums, brightly colored print displays promised the following variations on the theme "Great Gifts For Mom." (Borrowing an oft-repeated line from a fellow humorist, I *swear* I didn't make this up.)

• A banner copy line in a hardware store's sale insert read, "The Perfect Getaway for a Busy Mom!" Beneath that boast were "special-order-selections" including five different bathtub models, from whirlpool to the mundane enameled steel, four styles of shower enclosures, one-, two-, and three-handle tub/shower valves, and "to put safety first," a chrome bathtub grip, a blow-molded plastic bath bench, and a toilet guardrail.

(I could only imagine Kids and Spouse dropping hints about "the Perfect Getaway," which would immediately put my mind in tropical beach/moonlit seaside stroll/palm tree mode, then presenting me with a *bathtub* on Mother's Day? Any woman who could pull off a sincere-sounding, "Oh, my gracious, it's *just* what I've always *wanted*," deserves an Emmy more than Susan Lucci.)

• A "Savings and Special Values for Your Very Special Mom" promotion featured a hand-held vacuum cleaner ("has a special revolving brush to *really* dig out dirt!"), an eight-piece aluminum cookware set, an electric can opener ("it's a knife sharpener, too!") and a toaster which "raises and lowers toast"—as if poor little old me has had to make do all these years with the old-fashioned, windlass model.

Undoubtedly, ad writers (mostly guys—women wouldn't *do* this to their own kind) are the ones who decided Mother's Day and small appliances go together like Fritos and French onion dip. *Au contraire*, say I. Trust me: if "a new ten-speed blender" was a "Jeopardy" board answer, the correct question would *not* be, "How would nine out of ten mothers respond to Sigmund Freud's famous query, 'What does a woman want?' "

Although one circular did carry several pages of serious amethyst-to-diamond jewelry, the nittier-grittier Mother's Day suggestions were limited to:

• A "Your Choice, $12.99!" silver-plated trinket box, vanity tray, or vanity set.
• A "Your Choice, $19.99!" etched crystal wine set, fruit bowl, candy dish, or pitcher.

I had a feeling that although several of those gem-dandy pages had mysteriously appeared in briefcases, sock drawers, and beneath cereal bowls the preceding week, more moms received a silver-plated trinket box than received a pricey trinket to put *in* one.

However, my personal favorite was an ad spread simply titled "Great Gift Ideas" and illustrated with a heart-shaped cameo depicting a serenely posed mother and child.

The layout had variously sized, red-bordered boxes, containing, from left to right, a Thighmaster exerciser, a Portable Steppe, and a Body Slide. Beneath those was a list of case-priced discounts on Ultra Slim-Fast Powder and Ultra Slim-Fast Ready-to-Drink.

Completing this weight/health-conscious merchandising motif were an "easy-to-read" digital scale and a water-powered tooth cleaning machine, both offered at scintillating sale prices.

Gee, that's certainly what *I'd* want for Mother's Day—an assemblage of flab-fighting exercise equipment, diet dinners, a scale to prove how much I needed them, and an appliance designed to blast away food particles even though if I actually gave those low-cal liquids a try, the Water Pik pickin's would be *mighty* slim.

Considering the nifty gift ideas beaming back from Mother's Day sale brochures, is it any wonder that most women get some really cruddy loot thrust at them on the second Sunday in May?

And that's not even factoring in those dastardly fellas who buy their wives the power tools, fishing gear, and automotive accessories *they* didn't get for Christmas. Or those who empty-handedly murmur something like, "Darling, no store-bought present could mean as much as what you already have: a husband who loves you and two beautiful children." Which might tug heartstrings if Wife wasn't absolutely positive he'd had no *clue* that it was *that* Sunday again until their six-year-old surprised Mom with the teensy marigold sprout in a cut-off, half-pint milk carton she'd snuck home from school the preceding Friday.

I certainly can't speak for every Mother in America, but I darn sure know what *I'd* like to get on Mother's Day:

• A gift certificate from a housecleaning service that does floor-to-ceiling grime removal, then sprays everything in sight with a Teflon-like substance that permanently repels dust, fingerprints, Kool-Aid puddles, and grape jelly glops.

• A weekend at a spa where all staff members and guests are guaranteed to be ten years older, twenty pounds heavier, and 34 percent flabbier than I am.

• A really good book, a decanter of gourmet coffee, a basket of snacks with a heavy emphasis on things chocolate covered, a cushy lounge chair in a shady spot near a trickling stream, no bugs, and no one to bug *me* until "The End."

• Though world peace would be lovely, I'd settle for a day of domestic harmony when no sibling rivalries erupted. Come to think of it, if everyone got their own house orderly, even for just one day, we'd *have* world peace—wouldn't we?

• Dinner in a restaurant that has no child's menu, plus several hours spent dancing to Bee Gees, Hollies, Creedence Clearwater Revival, Johnny Rivers, and Roy Orbison songs in a club where the volume of same isn't equal to a turbojet engine's. Oh, and *not* being awakened the next morning by Scoobee Doo cartoons at 6 A.M.

Okay, so none of the above will likely ever be featured in a Mother's Day handbill, some are kind of expensive, and all have a lot more to do with pampering than practicality.

But hey, considering all she does to keep hearth, home, and hemisphere as evenly keeled as possible the other 8,736 hours a year, really, what besides pampering is a Mother's *one* day for?

So, hope does spring eternal, even as I hang up my new hummingbird feeder, slosh-wash the car, and polish my etched crystal cake plate, while attired in my new, pup-tent-sized muumuu.

House-Sold Words

While reading my local newspaper's "Homes for Sale" listings, I decided that if a Pulitzer Prize were given for Eternal Optimism, real estate advertising writers would win every time.

That isn't to say their intention is to deceive; it's more a nuance of the "If life gives you lemons, make lemonade" adage.

Therefore, even when a property's most saleable feature is the accuracy of the house numbers stenciled on the curb in front of it, the following real estate-oriented catchphrases are commonly used to attract a buyer's attention.

- *Health forces sale:* An unfortunate occurrence indeed if the current owner has a confirmed reservation at a nearby intensive care unit, but more likely, the deed holder is just damned sick and tired of living in that monument to Murphy's Law.
- *Open and airy:* The structure may lack sufficient insulation, so a steady breeze flows through every unchinked nook,

95

cranny, and electrical outlet within. Vestiges of this type of natural air-conditioning may also be present via all windows, doors, and potentially, the roof.

- *Fixer-upper:* Even Bob Vila would be supremely challenged to restore *this* old house.

- *Unlimited potential:* A skootch more hope for future habitation than in a "fixer-upper," but still a potential invitation to personal bankruptcy.

- *Needs some TLC:* Translates as "Needs Time, Lysol, and Cash"; the latter home-improvement loan preferably not secured from the institution carrying the original mortgage, which probably won't be willing to "go for broke" anyhow.

- *Owner moving out of state:* On the face of it, that clause may be true, but after the sale, *where* the current owner relocates may be dependent upon that locale's laws governing interstate extradition in cases involving misrepresentation and fraud.

- *Big garden spot:* In some cases, a backyard plot bounded on two sides by the septic tank's lateral lines. Because veggies are both watered and fertilized with every flush, maintenance is minimal and bumper crops are common.

- *Secluded:* Only a Jeep-equipped mail carrier and well-meaning folks representing various religious organizations have a snowball's chance in hell of finding you. But the peace and serenity of "getting away from it all" will wear off about the sixth time you have to make a forty-seven-mile round-trip just to pick up bread and milk because you forgot to buy them on the way home.

- *Motivated sellers:* Probably means they've already closed the loan on the house they're moving to, are now making double payments, and can't hold out much longer.

- *Country kitchen:* There's no guarantee this sought-after interior amenity features ducky-, lamby-, and bunny-print wallpaper with space available for hanging collectible antique farm implements. Don't be surprised to find that conversations echo off its rustic, mossy rock walls, that the stove reportedly uses very little firewood, and that the refrigerator is a convenient few steps away . . . on the back porch.

- *Must see:* In all probability, the listing real estate agent's contract is about to expire, and unless a few "live ones" tour it pretty soon, there's scant hope of a renewal.
- *Convenient location:* In addition to nearby shopping centers and schools, the fire department and ambulance service probably use this street for a shortcut.
- *Mature landscaping:* Tarzan, Cheetah, and Jane would feel very much at home amongst trees and bushes that haven't been trimmed since the Truman administration.
- *Earth-tone decor:* The carpeting, walls, and drapes are coordinated in varying shades of mud brown, harvest-moon orange, and tree-frog green, which creates the overall effect of sunset at the Okefenokee Swamp.
- *Dollhouse:* This cottage is spacious enough for Barbie and Ken's cohabitation, but Midge and Skipper'll have to get rooms at the Super 8 when they visit.
- *One-of-a-kind floor plan:* Yep, the contractor learned his lesson with *this* jewel.
- *All new paint inside and out:* The sellers got a great deal during a close-out sale at Billy Bob's Paint and Retread Tire Emporium—thirty gallons of assorted, custom-mixed colors for $2.99 each. Vat not included.
- *An architectural statement:* All other statements made by those previously shown this residence do not bear repeating.
- *Quality living areas:* Formerly known as "cozy" and definitely an antonym for "quantity." See dollhouse, above.
- *Full, dry basement:* Assuredly, those in the market for a house with a half, wet basement needn't bother looking.

• *Builder will consider trade:* The contractor's construction loan is due to balloon in a few days. He'll figure out what to do with your house later.

• *Priced below appraisal:* Either the original appraiser was shy a few batteries in his calculator, or he's the owner's sister-in-law's brother's son, or the owner is anticapitalism and therefore morally opposed to making a profit on his investment.

Whenever I've been in the market for a new or new-to-me residence, I've found that it pays to be a tad cynical about such there's-always-a-catch phrases. Since advertising is designed to shine the most flattering light on the property offered for sale, it's the buyer's job to put the "real" in "real estate."

One historical fact on supersalesmanship I've never forgotten: the Indian who sold Manhattan island was by no means an "ignorant savage."

Oh, the buyers surely had a knee-slappin' hoot telling their fellow Pilgrims how they'd pulled off the bargain of the century by paying a paltry $24 for the parcel . . . and it certainly *would* have been one whale of a deal if that tribesman had actually *owned* it.

So *caveat emptor,* kemosabe.

Doctor Doolittle, I Presume?

*f*or all the times I've snickered at Gene Autry's cinematic penchant for belting out ballads to his horse and/or herds of longhorns, I had no idea that Gene's lilting, livestock-oriented refrains weren't merely stupid, but may have had a profound psychological effect on his hoofed costars. Rather than chewing their cuds, those happy bovines might actually have been lip-syncing the words to those Singing Cowboy songs.

According to several newspaper articles I've read recently, the four-legged amongst us have similar emotional makeups, and therefore suffer the same psychoses that we do. Problem is, with the exception of Lassie and Mister Ed, animals have had no way of telling their troubles to highly trained, human members of the mental health community.

After all, even if a manic-depressive Doberman could paw his way to the proper yellow-paged section of the phone book, he'd have a heck of a time dialing the doctor's office— which is enough to make one wonder if intervention-seeking but digitally challenged pets are responsible for many of those "mystery" numbers that appear on monthly telephone bills.

The articles did reveal, however, that a Doctor Doolittle-ish alternative is available to diagnose and potentially cure these critters' mental and physical ills. Believe it or not, there are several animal psychics who specialize in using ESP to communicate with those unable to speak for themselves.

Even more amazing is that these diagnostic procedures can be done by telephone—with the animal's owner acting as a mediator—of course, of course.

Successfully resolved case histories included a chronically colicky horse whose gut-wrenching symptoms were psychically determined to be the result of "birth trauma." A series of phone consultations assuaged both the animal's "painful memories" and its tendency toward bellyaching.

An iguana's overaggressiveness was diagnosed (also via telephone) as acute sexual frustration. After introducing Mister Iguana (in person) to a cute lady lizard, nature took its course and—voilà—Mister Iguana was his old sweet self once again. (Oddly, Ms. Iguana's thoughts on being nothing more than a reptilian sex object didn't rate mention.)

In addition to their by-wire services, some practitioners also make barn calls for from-thine-muzzle-to-mine-ear psychic schmoozes. After one such confab with a severely dehydrated horse, the psychic was quoted as saying, "I kept tasting something chemical from the horse's mouth."

Although I absolutely do *not* want to know how that taint transference was accomplished, the animal's owner subsequently tested the stream running through Horse's pasture and, by jove, found out it was polluted by formaldehyde being dumped by a business upstream.

Isn't that incredible? I mean, who but a psychic could have *possibly* concluded that a horse's refusal to drink might be caused by a polluted water supply?

The cost of these extrasensory perceptions ranges from $35

to $135 each, in addition to, presumably, long-distance tolls and/or to-site travel expenses. While responding to the standard cocktail party inquiry, "And what do *you* do for a living?" by replying that one is an animal psychic, with patients ranging from urpy horses to exceptionally horny lizards, might set off some serious guffaws, the pay scale for such procedures is certainly respectable.

The proliferation of bow-bedecked, toenail-polished pooches and the annual sales figures for four-sleeved tuxedos, tutus, and après-ski wear testifies that millions of pet lovers have no qualms about putting their money where their mouth is when it comes to their beloved animal companions.

And, since livestock ownership represents a heavy-on-the-hoof investment for ranchers, it's understandable that when the local veterinarian can't cure Bossy's blue mood and it can't be sung into submission, a toll call goes out for psychic intervention.

But regardless of these nigh miraculous accounts, I doubt if I'll be dialing for a long-distance diagnosis of my dog's obsessive compulsion to bark at falling leaves, June bugs, wind currents, moon phases—absolutely *anything* except potentially homicidal strangers who appear unbidden at my doorstep.

Such skepticism prevents me from ever knowing whether that barkmeister is psycho or merely dumber than dirt, but I'd rather not risk having to explain that my telephone was busy all afternoon because Dog was feeling repressed and needed to reach out and whine at someone.

As the saying goes, since "Music hath charms to soothe the savage breast" (or hopefully *beast,* as it were), if I get unduly concerned about my pet's psyche, I'll go the cheaper—and probably just as scientific—route by popping a few CDs in the player and letting the Singing Cowboy croon that l'il doggie's cares away.

Terminal Phobia

Lots of people suffer from aerophobia—the fear of high objects or heights, specifically, a fear of flying. I, on the other hand, *enjoy* cruising along in the clouds.

It's airports that scare the bejesus out of me.

Much has been said about their being called "terminals," and that the word *memorial* appears in their names as often as it does in cemeteries'.

Obviously, not *enough* has been said about it or this custom would be a dead issue, so to speak.

Nor does my heart soar when the first thing I see upon entering these "memorials" is a bank of life-insurance vending machines lining the walls. The concept of buying a gob of life insurance (which is actually *death* insurance) in a place called a *terminal* adds a certain two-strikes-against-me *je ne sais quoi* to my attitude.

Though I suppose airport security departments can't be too careful, I seriously question whether my nearby, eight-gate-sized airport will ever be designated a top ten target for terrorism. But whether it's the local facility or others I've patronized, there's ample reason to doubt the veracity of high-tech metal detecting systems.

These alarms tend to scream bloody murder when honing in on some elderly woman's metal hosiery hooks, but don't beep a bit when the Marlboro man behind her strolls through the archway wearing a belt buckle the size of a baby moon hubcap.

Airport rest rooms pose another persnickety problem. As I found out when toting a garment bag as carry-on luggage—primarily so it and I had a reasonably good chance of deplaning on the same continent—while there are as many as fifty stalls aligned side-by-side like cattle chutes, their dimensions are about as roomy as a telephone booth.

My garment bag can fit inside. *I* can fit inside. But there's no way we can go together. Leaving my luggage outside the door seems a gilt-edged invitation for theft, so I must seek out what I hope is an honest-faced fellow passenger to guard my essentials while I answer the call of nature.

Beyond the bathrooms, there's a nest of food vendors offering all kinds of highly salted fare. The aroma of hot pretzels, sizzling Polish sausages, and pizza slices is nectar to my nose when I know a bag of peanuts is the only munchy I'll get en route.

However, partaking of these vended vittles requires a quart or so of thirst-quenching beverages as a chaser, so depending upon how much time remains before departure, I'll either have to suffer the small-stall routine again, or be predisposed to take a potty break at thirty-five thousand feet.

That an airplane comes equipped with a relief station is quite miraculous, but using it invariably results in an episode of "unexpected" turbulence and the heart-stopping dread that its door could jostle open during my enthronement.

Altitude and salt-inspired water retention also conspire to

swell my feet three sizes larger than my shoes. It's easy to spot similarly bloat-impaired passengers—we're the ones who toddle splay-footed out the arrival tunnel like Charlie Chaplin in *The Little Corporal.*

But the most phobia-inducing moments occur when the ticket checker by the boarding gate announces that my flight is overbooked and offers megabuck bounties to anyone willing to trade their ticket, and not one of the seventy-three people clutching confirmed boarding passes for the forty-two-seat plane so much as sneezes in response.

After a whispered consultation with another uniformed airlineperson, the checker cheerfully issues a preboard call for disabled passengers and those accompanied by small children, as if the aforementioned overload was just a bit of airline humor the staff felt compelled to share.

I'll admit, I've been desperate enough to ensure my seat that I've offered short-term lease arrangements on one of a harried mother's brood for long enough to get me past the boarding gate guard. And sometimes, it's even worked.

Once I've run these gauntlets on the ground, I'm too frazzled to give a rip how an enormous, megaton airship gets its tail aloft and keeps it there. That it *does* is enough for me . . . until the pilot announces that our destination is approaching.

As I feel that sinking-swaying sensation caused by decreasing altitude, my hands start sweating, my breath comes in pants, and it feels like the cabin temperature has risen about twenty degrees, and I wonder:

• Will my connecting flight's gate be in the same zip code that this plane will park in?

• If not, can I sprint to its departure gate at speeds approximating seventeen miles per hour while lugging a garment bag, briefcase, and purse? Will I qualify for the next Olympic Games if I do?

• Is there *any* doubt that the other flight will depart on time since this one's ten minutes late?

• Once on the ground, is it remotely possible that an in-working-order rest room will precede the zillion gift shops, foodmeisters, Irish-themed pubs, flower shops, and newsstands?

• If the arrival/departure monitors are on the blink, and the airline's information desk has nary a human behind it, who am I supposed to ask for a flight status report? The custodian?

• If I'm not traveling onward, assuming I can find the baggage retrieval area, will every piece of luggage riding the conveyor be identical to mine? Will the first ones I glom onto belong to the North American Surly Attitude Champion?

Afraid of flying? Hardly. There are only two things that can go wrong in the process: not getting off the ground or coming down prematurely. Neither happens often enough to really worry me, and I figure the day one does, it'll be my *last* cause for alarm, anyhow.

But there are at least a hundred and one fears feeding my phobia about airport terminals. And unfortunately, I don't think any of them are close to being *terminated*.

Whirled Traveler

ꝺon't think me blasphemous, but I know where heaven is—it's alone, away from home, nestled in a motel room with maid service, room service, a good book, a big bag of white cheddar popcorn, and absolute command of the television's remote control.

While I know those who spend more days on the road than at home might argue, Moms like me fairly *leap* at the chance to attend an out-of-town convention.

However, after several trips spent in the unrelenting bliss of do-what-I-wanna solitude, Murphy's Law (never known as Murphy's Suggestion) made me due for a downer.

It came in conjunction with a conference being held in Very Small Town, U.S.A., so the promotional brochure only listed a few convenient hostelries. As I dialed the first one's reservation number, its very name—the Water's Edge Motel—brought forth images of a quaint inn overlooking the Missouri River.

I envisioned the mom-and-pop establishment as offering an idyllic interlude, with music supplied by the riffling river's waters, perhaps a batch of freshly made muffins delivered to my door, and snowy-white linens crackling on a soft, oh-so-king-sized bed.

Reservation secured, I packed my bags and set out to take advantage of one of the self-employed's rare opportunities to combine a tax deductible perk with pleasurable rest and recreation.

But all my romantic renderings vanished the second I saw my temporary home away from home. The Water's Edge was so mustily decrepit, I assumed there must be a plaque somewhere proclaiming: LEWIS AND CLARK SLEPT HERE.

It was hardly a surprise to learn that this motel from hell was the only one in town with a flickering VA--N-Y sign. Naturally, the closest community with less rustic accommodations was an hour and a half's drive away.

Since misery loves company, I and several other seminar attendees decided we'd stick together, tough it out, and pay the owners forty-six bucks a night for the privilege of testing our mettle to the maximum.

After checking in, my room's Early Garage Sale decor, although fraught with chenille bedspreads and gold-speckled ceramic accessories, *was* clean and comforting in an Aunt Mildred's Sleeping Porch sort of way. What gave me pause was the unmistakable aroma of eau de Raid that slapped me in the sinuses the second I opened the door.

After considering the alternatives, I decided I'd rather coexist with a pall of pesticide than be greeted by the gargantuan cockroaches I imagined living behind the wainscoting.

Calling home to report my safe arrival proved a problem, too. Because the Water's Edge was undoubtedly built before Alexander Graham Bell was a twinkle in his mother's eye, there was no phone in my room. The phone booth in the parking lot, provided, as a sign read, "for the convenience of our guests," further informed that it was padlocked by the management at 9 P.M.

And the big hand on my watch sat at a dead-on 9:02.

I could see a television's glow strobing from the office's back room, but the owners were as deaf to my knock as they were to my muttered comments questioning their legitimacy.

As the night wore on, I can't say I hadn't seen the railroad trestle adjacent to the motel, but I also can't say I expected freight trains to roar over it so regularly. And other than the combination fire/ambulance/police departments' siren located across the street that cranked to life at one-hundred-and-twelve-minute intervals, presumably just to see if the damn thing still worked, the hours passed in relative peace.

However, the next morning when I was, to put it delicately—seated on the throne and minding my own business, I was practically launched from that humble stance when my next-room neighbor plopped onto *his* potty. Little did Neighbor know, every wiggle caused a corresponding convulsion to *my* commode, effecting a bizarre, two-toilet teeter-totter. Such rest room recreations quickly lent a new definition to the phrase "bowel movement."

My first thought was to immediately

dismount, except I couldn't figure out how to do so without sending shock waves through my seatmate's fixture. Thankfully, it must have been a slow news day, and my blissfully unaware cohort was not a crossword puzzle fan. Within minutes, I got the drift that removing my personage would not cause Neighbor any undue repercussions.

Showering was an adventure of a different stripe. Not only was the curtained stall elevated two steps higher than the rest of the room, its floor was covered with—judging by the distinctive Ford logo—a cut-to-fit floor mat. This not only illustrated the shower's compact dimensions, I shuddered to think what Management might have decided to hide beneath that hunk of black rubber.

About the time I felt the water level rising to above-ankle depths, I noticed the graceful waterfall it created as it cascaded over the stall's narrow lip, down the steps and onto the linoleum-covered dressing area.

Where the water went from there I didn't care to know, but it did recede rather quickly after I turned off the spigot.

Although any out-of-town accommodations, whether chain-style or privately owned, present a pig-in-a-poke proposition, my stay at the Water's Edge certainly established a Rule of Thumb for Road Travel that any wanderer should consider:

If a motel's brochure or billboard only advertises its enormous parking lot, shopping convenience, or kiddie swings/pool as amenities, *humbleness* on the part of the ownership probably has nothing to do with it.

Or, on second thought, humbleness may have *everything* to do with it.

On the Road Again

Occasionally, I put the mobility of my profession to the test. Though it's true that all a writer *really* needs to get the job done is paper, a pencil, and sufficient inspiration, we modern scribes are more accustomed to seeing our chosen words flickering on a computer monitor than flowing in blue ink across a ruled tablet.

But whenever an invitation for a day trip arises and I take my show on the road while my companion does errands and generally goes about business, I'll ferret out a comfortable, sort-of quiet niche, set up shop, and start committing thoughts to paper the old-fashioned way.

It never ceases to surprise me that a gal perched on a bench with notebook in lap and pen in hand, amidst a bustling shopping mall, can draw the attention of onlookers quicker than a car wreck.

And hard as I may try to concentrate on the plot or philosophy streaming through my consciousness, noticing with ever-alert peripheral vision that the same person has strolled in front of me a half-dozen times—and slowed the pace with each pass—never fails to distract me from my purple prose.

Most often, the prowler is an older gent whose curiosity has overcome his shyness. After making timid eye contact and finding me potentially friendly, he'll drawl an icebreaking remark such as, "Hey there, looks like you're workin' hard," or, "Mornin' young lady. D'ya mind my askin' what you're doing?" or "Say there, are you a writer?"

What follows is about five minutes of delightfully sociable chitchat. Upon confessing that writing is my profession, he'll likely admit how difficult spelling and English were for him back in those one-room school days. How he's never been much of a reader, except for newspapers, and how *they* weren't worth wrapping garbage in anymore. Then his eyes will twinkle mischievously and he'll grin as he says he's always loved a good story, and that, by golly, he's told a few ripsnorters himself in his time.

All the while, I'll sit and nod a lot and smile sincerely at this fascinating, nameless new friend I've made.

Soon, he'll run out of steam or maybe feel a twinge of guilt for keeping me from my muse. Or more likely, his wife will come between us.

With a blustery, maternal tone, she'll apologize for his intrusion, then turn and chastise him for jabbering to a stranger as if he were a boy of seven rather than a man of seventy.

Having learned long ago that fighting such marital city halls is fruitless, he'll look everywhere but at the woman pecking at him verbally, or the one holding a notebook and pen and feeling embarrassed for him.

Yet, even as the Missus leads him away, still lecturing between assorted clucks and "For heaven's sakes," he'll risk a backward glance and a conspiratorial wink—the latter of which I'll gladly return.

I'm not sure why, but such conversational interludes rarely

feature an elderly female costar. Women are equally inquisitive but, inexplicably, are much less likely to circle then pounce on my pursuits.

Instead, they'll park on an adjacent bench and stare, averting their eyes in a flash if I aim mine in their direction. Or they'll scrutinize me unblinkingly, as if I were sprouting a second head or probably "up to no good."

Perhaps as youngsters, we women learned that "Don't talk to strangers" prohibition entirely too well. Maybe, as many would likely insist, a lady is, above all, raised to mind her manners, and most would sooner wear white shoes before Easter or after Labor Day than make a nuisance of themselves. And Lord only knows, today's crime statistics don't encourage outbreaks of casual repartee.

Nonetheless, it's occurred to me that women of all ages deny themselves too many of life's *sit a spell* moments where nothing much happens except an acknowledgment that most folks you meet are not only harmless, but certainly worth knowing, even if it's only for a few minutes and even if you never learn their names.

I think it's a shame that most of the women I encounter on the road probably let these interludes pass for no better reason than the fear of making fools of themselves. In the meantime, their husbands are making a friend of a gal who's just sitting on a bench in a busy shopping mall, with pen in hand and balancing a notebook on her knees.

I'd always heard the best thing about traveling is the people you meet. And thanks to some gracious, gregarious gentlemen whose acquaintance I've made fleetingly, by golly, I'm here to tell you, it's *true*.

In Working Order

Never invest in anything that eats

or needs repairing.

BILLY ROSE

Timing Is Everything

-ʚ-
I f I had to pick a personal credo, it'd probably be "The hurrier I go, the behinder I get." As a busy mom and an admitted workaholic, I sometimes feel like the Mad Hatter's role model.

To cure my chronic crunch, I've studied numerous theories on time management. While many appeared quite profound on paper, they failed miserably during stress tests.

"Devising a master plan with goals deadlined for completion" sounded like a fine idea, at first. Like Santa Claus, I proceeded to make my list and check it twice.

And about a month later, I made confetti out of it after two kids breaking out with chicken pox, two others with car troubles who constantly absconded with my wheels or needed rides to work or school, a lightning strike that cremated all major household appliance innards, and unexpected houseguests obliterated any goal-tending hopes I'd had.

"Prioritizing personal and professional events, commitments, and plans" was supposed to help me get the big jobs done and let the piddlies twist in the wind—indefinitely, if need be. Except one person's priorities are often considered piddlies by someone else, and vice versa.

For example, running out of Honey Nut Cheerios was hardly an earthshaker to me, but to Younger Son, my lack of inventory control was tantamount to child abuse.

Conversely, one of my impending, business-related deadlines cast hardly a ripple in Son's mind—not with his allowance burning a hole in his pocket and an insatiable desire to peruse every discount store in town to find the best price on a Super Soaker squirt gun.

"Determine where your time is going" turned out to be an easy directive to follow: three hours were subsequently devoted to scribbling a six-page list of time takers, except I noticed that identifying them didn't exactly turn back the clock.

However, at least I now had copious notes to refer to during my next you-have-no-idea-how-much-you're-gonna-miss-me-when-I'm-gone speech.

According to the advice on "Identifying your time wasters," the most common are: indecision, lack of planning, jumping from one project to another, keeping a disorganized desk, procrastinating, and insisting on perfection.

That synopsized Life As I Know It in a mere twenty words, so I planned to start correcting the errors of my ways by cleaning my desk, except I also needed to return some phone calls and answer a few letters, and since I couldn't decide which was the Priority, I simply went to the kitchen and mixed a *perfect* Margarita.

"Stay focused" is a common command, with "if nothing else gets done, you'll at least accomplish the most important entry on your day's to-do list," lending a smidgen of forgiveness to those of us who habitually wander off track.

That seemed quite aspirational until a week passed with

numbers two through ninety-seven not only remaining on the list, but beginning to glare at me with a distinctively nyah-ne-nyah-ne-nyah-nyah attitude.

I really wish I could "assert myself," as time-management experts advise, but as the mother of four children, it should be fairly obvious that saying no is not one of my best things.

The final precept of many of these instructive commentaries is "get away from it all regularly" to rest and recharge weary internal batteries. Supposedly, by instituting the aforementioned techniques, enough spare time should be created to go bask in the Bahamas on a quarterly basis.

And if I believed *that*, I'd be a prime pigeon for any Florida swampland salesman.

However, all the clock/calendar-stretching techniques I've tried *did* teach me something, an unshakable belief in what I call:

LEDBETTER'S LAWS OF TIME MANAGEMENT

1. Almost everything takes longer to accomplish than you think it will.

2. Things that are accomplished promptly will have to be done over for one stupid reason or another.

3. A day is composed of only fourteen hundred and forty minutes, but there are usually twenty-eight hundred and eighty things that need doing during one.

4. Regardless of how many tasks *do* get done, only those that *don't* will be noticed. And the noticees will be sort of miffed about it. But not miffed enough to lift a finger to help.

5. People with nothing to do all day don't get the flu. Nor do their family members.

6. Those who complain loudest about eighteen-hour work-

days, poor working conditions, and an overly demanding boss are probably self-employed.

7. When others say they were "too busy" to get something done, it actually means they were just too lazy. But when *you* say you were too busy, you really *were* too busy.

8. The longer the list of to-dos, the harder it will be to find time to start them.

9. Just when you think you're going to get everything done and finally have time to relax, a catastrophe rears its ugly head. By the time it's resolved, you're farther behind than you were when you started.

10. The same three hours that fly by when you're on a deadline seem like an eternity when you're waiting for an important telephone call.

Considering all the "expert" how-tos I've tried and tossed, plus the effects of Ledbetter's Laws of Time Management, I think I'm better off sticking with my own Timex-style rule for playing Beat the Clock.

By liberally applying perseverance, patience, and a sense of humor to my shortcomings, by golly, most days I can take a lickin' and keep on tickin', too.

You Know It's Gonna Be a Bad Day When . . .

The shower runs out of hot water just about the time your head's completely sudsed with shampoo. And after risking chilblains while rinsing the bubbles out, a foot-square facecloth is all you find in the linen cabinet to dry off with.

You're apprised of a panty hose manufacturer's definition of a "slight irregularity" when the waistband of a bargain-priced pair stretches to your collarbones while the crotch remains at about knee-level.

The customer who occupied the restaurant booth before you undoubtedly devoured a short stack of pancakes for breakfast, leaving behind several souvenir drips of maple syrup, which have now glued your brand-new silk shirt's left sleeve to the tabletop.

Your mother-in-law telephones to ask your opinion on redecorating the living room of her new house. When you remark that such remodeling is certainly needed since the former owner's peony-print wallpaper and striped curtains are the godawfullest combination you've ever seen, you're curtly informed that those were the only two items she hadn't planned on changing.

In the process of carefully applying a stroke of liquid eyeliner, a sudden sneeze sends the wand skidding toward your right ear, which creates that lovely, water-resistant, I-just-went-six-rounds-with-Rocky look.

After strictly adhering to a new roots-and-berries-only diet, the scale informs you that you've gained three pounds.

The milk you're pouring over your morning granola has a decidedly chunky consistency.

After lunching with a business associate, the waiter snottily informs you that your credit card didn't clear and you know you have a grand total of $1.13 in cash in your billfold.

The good news is, for once, that you're ready to leave home in plenty of time to make a scheduled appointment, but the bad news is that the trash truck has picked the end of your driveway as the perfect place to drop its transmission.

Striding toward the podium to give a talk to a local civic organization, you feel the sinking sensation of your bra coming unhooked, which immediately puts a whole new spin on the concept of "free speech."

With a styling brush held in the exact position your hairdresser used to blow-dry some body into your decidedly limp hair, you can't get the $%^&^* bristles to let *go* again. And you doubt if anyone will believe the brush is a trendy new kind of barrette.

After unsympathetically diagnosing your child's morning headache as a bad case of biology-final flu as opposed to actual flu flu, she promptly loses her breakfast all over the hallway carpet, which makes you feel worse than she does.

Starting the car to warm it on a cold winter's morning, you not only accidentally lock the keys inside *it*, you soon discover that you've also locked yourself out of the house. And of course, no one else is home. That'd be too easy.

You can't get the zipper zipped on your "fat" jeans.

After heaping two grocery carts with enough provisions for a month's menus and munchables, then piling said supplies on the supermarket's conveyor, you open the checkbook and find a deposit slip staring you in the face.

You go to wake up your teenager and find that the bed hasn't been slept in.

Having been instructed to fill out a hotel registration card, though you think you've excavated a pen from the bottom of your purse, the tubular object with which you find yourself trying to sign the "guest's name" line turns out to be a regular absorbency tampon.

Planning to wear a winter white outfit to a cocktail party, you don a robe while applying your makeup and don't dare even to sip on a cola in the process in order to avoid accidental spills. You may even wash your hands before slipping into and buttoning the garment to lessen the possibility of smudges. After congratulating yourself on such pristine and careful grooming, you then slam the car door shut on your skirt.

Neighbor calls just before breakfast to give you the entire play-by-play of yesterday's ingrown toenail operation.

Desperate to get a due-today bill postmarked accordingly, you arrive at the post office only to discover that it's Arnold T. Horselax's birthday and the facility is closed up tighter than a (supply your own analogy).

You spot the only two remaining parking spaces on the mall's two-acre lot, and by the time you get there some jerk driving a fancy sports car has already angled across both of them. After leaving a scathing note relating your opinion of such #$&^% behavior, you'll later learn that the vehicle belongs to the new chief of police's wife.

The deejay on your favorite radio station announces that he's just chosen your name at random and if you call the station within five minutes, you'll win a ten day, all-expenses-paid cruise to the Bahamas. After bashing three toes into the bedpost in your haste to get to the phone, the line is inexplicably deader than Dillinger. For six minutes.

You're salivating just thinking about snarfing the box of frozen gourmet Belgian waffles you've stashed away in the back of the freezer, and all you'll find is the empty carton.

Upon awakening the kids for the first of day school following Christmas vacation and subsequently, five consecutive snow days, each in turn moans, "Mommy, I don't feel so good."

I suppose it could be said that sometimes it *really* doesn't pay to get up in the morning. Except, chances are, the day you decided to stay burrowed beneath the covers for the duration, your lifetime-guaranteed waterbed mattress would start geysering like Old Faithful.
Which would short out its electric heater.
Which would send sparks shooting from the outlet.
Which would catch the drapes on fire . . .

1,987,432 (More or Less) Labor-Saving Devices No Home Should Be Without

$\mathcal{S}$ peaking as one who still considers a microwave oven a major miracle, and who has, in ten years, hardly advanced beyond reheating coffee and zapping bowls of canned soup, I am absolutely astounded by the number and variety of highly specialized household gadgets gleaming from store shelves today.

It seems that small-appliance manufacturers are spawning products faster than guppies hatch in an aquatically correct environment. But despite aisle upon aisle of shiny chromium carrying lofty claims, I couldn't imagine myself lugging any of these corded contraptions *home*.

In the first place, equipping my kitchen with gee-whizzy geegaws ranks just above "training to become a hod carrier" on my What I'd Most Like to Do in My Spare Time list.

Secondly, on closer inspection, I decided that most of them would likely wind up as grist for a future garage sale.

For example, an automatic bread maker, which was approximately the size of a portable color television, promised "light, fluffy loaves just like Grandma used to make."

My hips widened just thinking about those soft, steaming slices slathered with butter or honey. But I know darned good and well the only reason *my* grandmother was up to her earbobs in bread dough on a weekly basis is because sliced, store-bought loaves weren't available until the thirties. As soon as the ready-to-eat stuff hit grocery store shelves, she said sayonara to *that* chore in a heartbeat.

A juice extractor was another large "small" appliance I'd not seen before. According to blurbs on its box, the machine was designed to squash every drop of liquid from all kinds of fresh veggies and fruits into one container, while it simultaneously urped the pulp into another. What the owner was supposed to do with glops of juiceless, pulp by-products was probably explained in its numerous paged operations manual.

Though I supposed those extractions were quite healthful, and presumably economical, I seriously doubt if maiming a few pounds of produce will ever be part of my daily routine.

The food steamer/rice cooker's function was pretty self-explanatory, except I already have a piece of kitchen equipment that does the same thing. It's called a "lidded saucepan."

Yet these gizmos were only the first in a l-o-n-g line of kitchen wizardry promising to save me loads of domestic labor, such as:

- Electric potato bakers—not to be confused with potato curler/cutters, or potato peelers, or potato chip makers.
- Iced-tea pots (ice not included), hunkered beside a dozen different styles of percolators, coffee makers, coffee grinders,

and espresso/cappuccino cookers. In the case of the latter, oddly enough, brewing a teensy, two-ounce cup of high-falutin' coffee requires a huge, pressurized, steam-belching behemoth that, in operation, sounds like a B-52 preparing for takeoff.

• One-at-a-time tortilla bakers, which look a lot like grid-less waffle irons and would certainly afford diners plenty of opportunity for siestas between servings.

• Electric knife sharpeners, guaranteed to keep one's cutlery honed to their lethal limits. Note: might not be needed by the proud owner of an electric vegetable/fruit peeler, an electric vegetable/fruit mincer, and/or an electric vegetable/fruit slicer.

• Bazooka-like utensils one is supposed to load with the lettuce and various other salad-oriented ingredients, which are then fired into a salad bowl. A container enormous enough to keep the operator from sending shredded greenery shrapnel everywhere but at the intended target is not included, but is likely recommended.

• Electric ice chippers/sno-cone makers—a must for every household that contains a recovering tonsillectomy patient or enjoys building daiquiris from the ice up.

• Food grinders (obviously a more specialized version of food processors with a grinding attachment), which come complete with a "pusher" for, presumably, prodding reluctant vittles into those whirling, stainless steel jaws and a "sausage stuffer" for aiding in the production of myriad porcine treats that few folks have a low enough cholesterol count to consume anymore, anyway.

Plus: blenders, food processors, hand mixers, stand mixers (with quite lethal looking attachments), toasters, convection oven/grills, meat marinaders, pasta makers, ice cream freezers, toaster ovens, deep fryers, hot hamburger broilers, hot dog cookers, bun warmers, food dehydraters, grinders, skillets, bag sealers, popcorn poppers, egg poachers, and combination griddle/warming trays.

Despite a what-could-they-possibly-come-up-with-*next?* attitude, as I perused the seemingly endless array I knew that by Christmas a new herd of mechanical doodads would hit the market, primarily for gift giving to those adjudged to have everything except, by George, a two-speed, electric berry stemmer.

I could not for the life of me understand why anyone would want a bevy of these reputed labor-saving devices. Ownership would require no less than several acres of counter or cupboard space to display or store them, and most came with numerous components that not only didn't wash and dry themselves, but were rarely deemed dishwasher safe.

Then, I realized that for *precisely* those reasons, buying several dozen small appliances really would save me some *major* daily labor.

The way I figure it, once my kitchen is completely equipped with both large "small" and small "small" appliances, we'll be eating out three, maybe four nights a week, at least.

After all, with all those contraptions crammed in the cabinets, how much room could I possibly have left for *food?*

It's All Geek to Me

As a lifelong member of the KISS (keep it simple, stupid) segment of society, I didn't acquire a computer to cruise the "information highway," or extrapolate income tax data, or even electronically annihilate invading space aliens.

Despite the jillion gee-whizzy things I knew a computer was capable of doing, all I wanted was a turbotypewriter. Suffice it to say, pursuing a keyboard-intensive career had done nothing to raise my speed/error ratio above that of an arthritic stork's. Rather than remaining the primary market for the makers of Wite-Out, I wanted a machine with word processing prowess—by my definition, equipment to raise my "F u cn rd ths" stenography-school-style technique to something resembling actual English.

Other than a smidge of that heart-thumping apprehension any credit card holder feels while awaiting the Master's approval of a multizeroed purchase, *buying* a computer was easy. Operating same proved to be something else (*read: what it was is profoundly unprintable*).

The computer store's salesperson had snidely assured me that the software he installed was appropriate for users like me who don't know RAM from ROM and sincerely don't give a damn if they ever do. But regardless of my request for a program designed for the "eighteen months and older" set, the operator's manual was crammed with instructions like:

> This command is useful if you want to convert EXE files to binary format. The file named by filespec is the input file. If no extension is specified, it defaults to EXE. The input file is converted to COM file format (memory image of the program) and placed in the output file. If you do not specify a drive, the drive of the input file will be used.

Because the manual's entire 721-page contents reflected its writer's Ph.D. in Geekspeak, I figured I'd have a better chance of translating the Dead Sea Scrolls than getting much beyond the book's table of contents. However, an 800-number "Help Hotline" promised human assistance to the severely computerese-impaired.

During our toll-free conversation, the consultant bandied about terms such as *auto exec bat, memory-resident software, exporting data,* and *downloading,* whereas my replies remained a consistent "Huh?"

This fascinating repartee could likely have gone on for hours had the consultant's mother not insisted he take his afternoon nap.

In desperation, I sought the guidance of a bilingual buddy— a fellow fluent enough in Geek to get the instructions' drift, then explain same to me in everyday American.

Buddy gleefully tampered with my CONFIG.SYS (whatever *that* is) to alter the software to suit my minimal needs, while I jotted crib notes listing the key sequences necessary to make the machine do my bidding.

For example, the manual had devoted ten pages of unintelligible drivel to detailing how to back up files by zipping them from the hard disk onto a floppy.

Buddy's oral description of this process claimed about three minutes.

My version boiled down to: "Copy files = C:\ copy *.* A:." Definitely, a KISS of dearth.

Once my just-the-facts-ma'am notes were complete and I was flying solo, the only glitches I encountered were random, monitor-flashed messages like "Error Reading in Drive C! Abort, Retry, Fail."

Those options did seem a smidge negative—if not potentially disastrous—yet that mechanical mayday always reminded me of the dorky robot on "Lost in Space" flailing its pneumatic arms and whining "War-ning! War-ning!"

Nor did the keyboard's "Help" key provide enough aiding and abetting. Activating that function resulted in my monitor screen filling with unintelligible crud when all I usually needed was a simple yes or no answer. To receive that simplified response, I was forever phoning Buddy for consultation.

No doubt, if only the keypad could have been rewired so whenever I pressed "Help" Buddy's phone rang automatically, I'd have devised a *truly* user-friendly function.

But for the most part, I was turbotyping quite contentedly until word got around that "I'd joined the twentieth century" equipmentwise. Immediately, several computer-adept acquaintances conspired to complicate my preschool-level program.

With levels of enthusiasm not seen since the United States

Hockey Team wiped the ice with their Russian counterparts, a veritable swarm of Geeks descended upon my office.

Attempts to refuse such well-meant efforts proved impossible. To them, using but a fraction of a computer's capabilities should be a punishable offense carrying a five-hundred-dollar fine and up to ten days in jail. Repeat offenders would be taken out and shot.

As each unwanted, exceptionally high-tech, mindboggling boondoggle was being "loaded," the Geek loading it gushed, "Just wait'll you get this *pièce de résistance* up and running—trust me, you'll *love* it!" in a tone reminiscent of a gourmand extolling the virtues of something supposedly foodlike, such as fricasseed eel parts, to someone of the decidedly peanut-butter-and-jelly persuasion.

Because compromise is the most intelligent resolution to a disagreement—particularly one you know you've got not a snowball's chance in hell of winning—I let them have their way with my machine. And after they left, blissful ignorance would reign supreme: I'd remain blissfully ignorant of all the electronic propaganda lurking in my computer's memory, and the Geeks would remain blissfully ignorant of my ignorance.

Except I had no idea how many aftereffects such multiperson piddling could create, including:

- The evaporation of numerous files into, presumably, the Black Hole. (Were any of them backed up on floppies? Get real.)
- Frequent system "hiccups," causing the machine to inflict touches of symbolism, such as ^^|<>@~&*|#$$%~~ @#&$^%%#*(&$&, smack in the middle of my peerless prose.
- Series of extremely rude electronic razzberries, alerting me to I knew not what.

• Intermittent lockups, which effectively glued the winking cursor in place on the screen, which this cursee had no clue how to unstick other than (a) rebooting the entire system or (b) putting a boot *through* the entire system.

Like most things in life, it took longer to undo the amok running through my computer's memory than it had for hacker-happy acquaintances to muck it up in the first place.

But to be fair, my software-sharing colleagues' intentions were good, and I really did appreciate their generosity, regardless of the results.

However, as a public service to prevent other KISS devotees from suffering similar snafus, allow me to pass on the following words of hindsighted wisdom: If staying low-tech is your highest ambition, *never* let anyone horse around with your computer—and be *especially* wary of Geeks bearing gifts.

It Ain't Happy Hour When It's Your Career on the Rocks

*C*alifornia has earthquakes. Florida gets wracked by hurricanes. We in middle America have tornadoes to contend with.

My corner of Missouri was long ago dubbed "tornado alley"—hardly a distinction bandied about by the Chamber of Commerce or Board of Realtors.

During my childhood, I spent many a spring day crouched beneath my school desk during tornado drills. At the time, I couldn't figure out *why* we were practicing avoidance techniques. I thought a twister was a one-way ticket to Oz, and hobnobbing with Munchkins would have at least gotten me out of washing the dinner dishes for a day or two.

I later developed a heartfelt respect for Mother Nature's frightful funnels when I watched one jitterbug through a residential neighborhood, leaving little besides kindling, shredded insulation, and uprooted trees in its wake.

Eventually, with four children feathering the nest, warnings of a tornado in the vicinity put *me* in protecor mode. Depending on which house we lived in at the time, my children might find themselves stacked like cordwood in a bathtub with a comforter draped across its top, or herded off to a safe niche in the basement.

I wish I could claim my role as defensive Mama Bear (Papa was rarely at home when the sirens started howling) was carried out with calm, organized efficiency.

Instead, when the power failed, and it usually did, I always had to cannibalize one of my kid's toys for flashlight-sized batteries, then interrogate said children to find out *who* snitched the flashlight from under the kitchen sink, and whereinthehell had he/she *left* it?

Latching onto a battery-equipped radio to track the storm's progress provided more search and seizure opportunities, but one of the kids usually got us broadcast functional before I had an actual seizure.

Naturally, by the time all emergency equipment was assembled and all minors were safely bunkered, the crisis had passed. But if the sirens had sounded in the middle of the night, the children were entirely too pumped with adrenaline to go back to bed.

Popcorn parties while watching circa-1944 black-and-white cowboy movies on television at three A.M. is the price this mom paid regularly for her tornado consciousness.

When I started writing for a living about a decade ago, I eventually cadged newly wedded Older Daughter's second-story bedroom for my home office. It wasn't until the first thunderous squall of the season reared its ugly head that I questioned the shrewdness of pursuing a paper-oriented career in such a lofty, and presumably tornado-attractive, location.

Nightmares of hundred-mile-an-hour-wind damage being wrought on my home in general suddenly took second place to those specifically featuring reams of paper with articles- and books-in-progress being shredded and scattered like confetti from hither to yon.

Though it never happened, that imminent possibility sent me scrambling to the basement wielding armloads of files and computer disks more times than I can count.

Then, last year, when the Stuff of My Writer's Life outgrew my home's available space, I moved the tonnage to an *honest to God* office complete with a fax machine and a degree of peace and privacy I certainly hadn't had at home.

And I was as contented as a clam in my digs until my best friend called one morning to inform me that one honkin' hail thrower of a storm was heading my way. A hasty radio weather check confirmed that the entire county was under a tornado watch. Conditions indicated that an upgrade to tornado warning status was a distinct probability.

Only then did it dawn on me that the office space I occupied was, again, dead-bang in the upper, southwest corner of a two-story building. And according to rumor and the National Weather Service, tornados have a habit of traveling from a southwesterly direction.

Worse yet, the forty-odd files for the book I was writing hadn't been "backed up" on disks—a security measure any half-smart computer user is supposed to perform daily. So, all I had to show for three months' work was a very vulnerable stack of paper and it was already lightninging too heavily to risk a fast, disk-copying job.

Pretty much panic-stricken, I grabbed the manuscript and started scrounging around for a tornado-proof place to stash it. But the file cabinets sat too near the windows. Ditto the bookcases, my desk, and every other sturdy piece of furniture I considered.

Spying the office's full bath rekindled Mama Bear memories. I was about to toss the papers into the tub, cover them with my person, then pray that if the good Lord spared them *and* me, from that day forward, I'd *never* procrastinate putting my irreplaceable files on easily protected disks, *ever again*.

In a flash, desperation spawned an alternative. I couldn't recall ever seeing a refrigerator bashed to bits by tornadic winds—sent skittering through a wall maybe, but not reduced to rubble. So, quick like a bunny, I zipped the manuscript into a garbage bag and chucked that precious bundle atop the heap of lunch-sized pizzas and Dilly Bars in the freezer.

I'm delighted to report that my fridge-as-tornado-vault theory wasn't put to the test. If it had, and I'd been wrong about that major appliance's invincibility, the book you're now reading would have probably have become little more than a blown-to-smithereens memory . . . and for me, anyway, one that wouldn't have been even the least little *bit* funny.

Packing It In

What I pack for an out-of-town business trip is wholly dependent on my mode of transportation.

If driving to my destination, I'm limited only by the interior dimensions of my seven-passenger van. And if it had come equipped with a trailer hitch, I'd schlepp about everything I own, including favorite home furnishings.

Air travel puts a crimp in my conglomerating because being able to lift my luggage is of supreme importance. There are few things more embarrassing than wrestling an Orca the Whale–sized duffel bag smack in the middle of a crowded airport concourse, and, to the amusement of those dawdling nearby, losing the Battle of the Bag by about three falls out of four.

I've also cringed when watching airline luggage loaders attempting to hoist it into a cargo bay. Those poor fellows' faces flush beet red just before they drop to their knees on the tarmac. For this, my garment bag has been nicknamed, by bag-persons from coast-to-coast, the "Widowmaker."

At the recommendation of other oft-flying females, I

invested in a collapsible luggage cart (training wheels for my garment bag) and a suitcase with a built-in handle and dual-wheels.

While I learned in a hurry that the former's elastic security strap was capable of pinching the bejesus out of the strapee's fingers, it seemed to do a pretty good job of making the Widowmaker mobile.

Then, during its maiden voyage—a business trip to Minneapolis (whose airport's baggage claim station is, undoubtedly, in St. Paul), I found out the hard way that my wheelie-dealie was *not* built for speed.

About the time I hit my stride, the Widowmaker started rocking to and fro as it rolled. On about the fourth fro, it lurched leftward on its side and laid there like an upended turtle.

Tugging cart and cargo upright caused the pull handle to semi-collapse, which caused the strap to detach, which heaved the bag in the opposite direction and completely off its wheelie-dealie.

To say I felt a tad conspicuous getting my gear together smack-dab in the middle of an extremely high traffic concourse is to say Jeffery Dahmer had a mild eating disorder.

As per the wheeled suitcase, being yoked in front of it and the mobile Widowmaker lent a greater sense of appreciation for the ox teams who yanked those Conestogas cross-country a century ago.

When used singularly, though I chose it specifically for its roominess, proliferation of pockets, and its maker's assurance that it would fit inside an airplane's overhead compartment, once that sucker was full, Arnold Schwarzenegger couldn't have hiked it above his knees.

Granted, such overloading isn't helped by the fact that my favorite casual ensembles (and some dressier ones) are anchored by jeans and boots—apparel known for durability, not feather lightness.

And I'll admit, recently hauling a sizable supply of same to a business conference not only strained a variety of internal organs, I was the *only* passenger whose luggage was denied transport on the final leg of the journey due to the plane's bad weather weight restriction. (Other conventioneers found that incident quite humorous. I was not one of them.)

But even when I leave that country-style attire behind, pound for pound, a female's gotta-haves outweigh a male's by about eight to one. At the minimum, we shes have to take cosmetics, hair-care products and appliances, a satchel of jewelry, shoes, belts, maybe a scarf or two, probably an extra purse, pajamas, underwear, and outerwear ranging from everyday to cocktail attire. And that's before I even *think* about "just in case" stuff.

I've read magazine articles that routinely tout "Get 191 Outfits from Only Five Mix-and-Match Separates." But while algebra is hardly my forte, the premise of those pieces sounds a skootch shy of doable.

First, such how-tos assume I'm willing to wear the same clothes for days on end. Even if I were, during about the second luncheon meeting, I'd *definitely* slop taco salad into my lap, thus wiping out a couple of garments critical to prolonged mix/matchability.

Conversely, a man can live on the road for weeks with little more than a shaving kit, a couple of pairs of slacks, jeans, shirts and ties, one all-purpose sport coat, a belt (reversible), and take-him-anywhere loafers.

A guy can sleep in his underwear, wash his hair with the same soap he showers with, and after a quick combing, let it air dry. And he can go from Laid-back to Dressy by merely slipping on a jacket and tie.

Fellas can travel so lightly, I presume that's where the term *briefcase* originated: with a few pairs of briefs stashed inside, a man's pretty much set for a three-day business trip.

Despite the Five Items = One Hundred Ninety-One Outfits Theory and garment industry advertising to the contrary, my clothes simply don't respond well to the hotel sink rinsings and drip dryings needed for subsequent rewearing. They may be rendered relatively clean, but I usually don't have an extra ten or twelve hours to stand around in the bathroom blasting them with my blow-dryer.

Unlike their masculine counterparts, women's clothing is also made of extremely wrinkle-challenged fabric. While much of my wardrobe carries "never needs ironing" labels, they emerge from the Widowmaker looking as if they'd been stomped on by the entire Kansas City Chiefs' offensive line.

Oh, I've tried the standard "hang them near a steamy shower" trick to release the wrinkles. More often than not, that's resulted in ickily damp, totally limp, and still grossly corrugated ensembles.

And it's infuriating to slither into one of the aforementioned for a Friday morning seminar and find myself standing beside a fellow who's been wearing the *same* three-piece pin-striper since Tuesday and is as sharply creased and natty as a model in a *Gentleman's Quarterly* advertisement.

Even if I get a firmer handle on packing light, that gotta-haves gender disparity will remain. For that reason alone, it wouldn't surprise me if there's a link between the lots-heavier tonnage we shes *have* to take along during out-of-town trips and many career women's penchant for working out every day after work.

All things considered, I figure that unless a gal can pump enough iron to bench press a Toyota, she probably has no *business* traveling.

Keep It at Fifty-five

I've noticed that even couples who have everything in common except ancestors get into snits over whose biological thermostat will be heeded at home.

If the he of the house wins, *she* will dress, day and night, in enough outerwear to scale Mt. Everest. If she prevails, *he'll* seldom be seen wearing much more than a pair of jockey shorts and a scowl.

Because Spouse is convinced that "Keep It at Fifty-five" is not only a speed-limit reminder but a catchy thermostat slogan, our home's average temperature, winter and summer, is nothing if not consistent, and can be summed up in one word: *cold*.

The only time the heat goes up is when I remark that although there's only a half inch difference in our heights, the sixty or so extra pounds of insulation *he* carries on *his* frame would keep *him* cozy in an igloo.

This climatic diversity made me peevish enough in the daytime, but I worsened appreciably at bedtime. Over the years, as the thermostat's setting *decreased*, the size and density of my nightwear *increased* proportionately.

From honeymoon frilly, I advanced to flannel, and then fleece. Suffice it to say, if floor-length fur was doable, I'd have given that a whirl, too.

It was never enough for Spouse that the furnace was our least-used household appliance. Even when icicles were dangling from the eaves, the bedroom window (located on my side of the bed, of course) had to be open "a crack": i.e., gaping enough to set the drapes dancing.

While I welcomed this "fresh air" concept on hot summer nights when the air-conditioning was in overdrive, there aren't enough quilts on the North American continent to stave off arctic breezes bent on blasting the hide off my backside.

Thankfully, before I froze or Spouse fried, I discovered a solution to these connubial chilblains and fevered blisters.

With a bit of basement beam bracing and the application of a couple of hundred gallons of lukewarm hosewater, we're now drifting off to dreamland upon the high seas—reposed passengers aboard a super deluxe QE II water bed.

It's approximately the size of Noah's Ark and came equipped with an enormous mirrored canopy which embarrasses the heck out of our children, but entertains the grandchildren when they bounce on the bed like a trampoline.

Naturally, progress did extract a price: there *are* a few user-unfriendly traits indigenous to surf snoozing.

For example, when Spouse thrashes about in his sleep, the resulting tidal turbulence can reach small-craft warning proportions. A death-grip on the side rails and a supply of anti-motion-sickness potions on the nightstand has helped me go with the flow. Only when already nauseated by the flu, a water-bed partner's *breathing* is enough to send this crew member tottering off to the toilet.

Due to the proximity of the heater coil, using the underbed storage drawers to stash chocolate snacks isn't a good idea

unless one prefers chocolate-covered peanuts as a beverage. Nor is taking a book to bed since sitting upright—and *staying* that way—is complicated by a mattress that's either continually ebbing and flowing or sinking slowly beneath the reader's buttocks.

For one who thought folding sets of standard sheets on a par with origami, attempting the same with waterbed coverings proved utterly impossible. Because their flat tops are securely stitched to their bottom-fitted counterparts, I have to wrestle with a bale of percale big enough to rig an America's Cup entry.

And the frustration of slopping four corners of, basically, a gargantuan, rectangular water balloon into the bottom sheet's corresponding pockets is second only to the infuriation of lying down and feeling that unmistakable *thwump* as each corner comes unhitched again.

Yet, for all the quirks of flotation-style slumber, I haven't missed our chilly innerspring bed one bit. And while Mr. Warmth has cranked the furnace's dial back to mid-Siberian range, I couldn't *be* more comfy.

Not with me and the water bed's thermostat sharing an identical temperature setting: a delightfully balmy 98.6 degrees.

The Strictly C-Food Diet Plan

I debuted this life at a statistically slight five pounds and change. Unfortunately, like most females, my weight has fluctuated appreciably from that day forward.

During my tomboyish childhood, I could eat anything I wanted without plumping my stickperson frame one whit. But during high school, my figure took on "chunky" proportions before I realized the old metabolism wasn't what it used to be. Somehow, puberty had changed my internal calorie combustion engine into a long-term fat-storage unit.

A few years later, the scales groaned in agony when I heaved all one hundred and eighty-five pounds of me onto them. I almost convinced myself that I was not really overweight but merely undertall, but eventually acknowledged that the odds of growing another twenty-seven inches or so were a lot slimmer than I was. A combination of dieting and exercise was the only alternative.

Except each of the dozens of eating plans I tried featured entrées that didn't exactly tickle my taste buds. No amount of cottage cheese, low-fat yogurt, or wafer-sliced bread satisfied my tummy's yen for a chili dog. A veritable troughload of lettuce (sans salad dressing), rice cakes, broasted turkey breast, and enough water to swamp the Queen Mary couldn't satisfy my hankering for a double-cheese pizza, French fries, and bowls of butter brickle ice cream.

Rather than deny myself the pleasures of the palate forever, I decided to stoke the old calorie furnace by exercising.

Granted, I *did* lose a few pounds, but I was much better at finding excuses *not* to exercise than I was at doing them.

- After reading an article that claimed jogging made breasts sag faster, I sold my running shoes at a garage sale.
- A neighbor told me that sit-ups were a leading cause of lower back problems. To my mind, a svelte silhouette wasn't worth the risk of putting a hitch in my get-along.
- Aerobics were terrific for those with good rhythm, but as a mother of four, I hardly counted *that* as one of my attributes.
- Swimming sounded doable until I found out the instructor expected me to do *laps* instead of dog-paddle in the baby pool.

However, I did begin to notice that simply mothering the aforementioned four children was doing wonders for whittling my waist, hips, and thighs—which was only fair since multiple pregnancies were what had caused many of my figure flaws in the first place.

Dandling a baby on one hip, slinging a diaper bag and my purse over the other shoulder, and dragging the other three children crack-the-whip-style through the mall toned muscles I didn't even know I had.

As my thundering herd grew, they invariably ran in only one direction: away. And before I could capture their attention, I had to capture *them*.

147

Plus, although by virtue of size, my children were built much lower to the ground than I was, the neverending chore of picking up everything from lock blocks to storybooks had become my Lot in Life. Suffice it to say, Einstein couldn't have calculated the number of toe touches and deep-knee bends I did every day.

However, despite the fact that I was getting more exercise than a marathoner, I still needed an eating plan that satisfied my food cravings without overloading my calorie intake.

Historically, the weight reduction regimens I'd tried hadn't cut the mustard for me, so I invented one geared to my likes and my life-style. While it might be a nutritionist's nightmare, since most of my favorite foods all begin with the letter C: cola, cheese, crackers, coffee, cauliflower, cheddar popcorn, celery, cereal, cherry cobbler, cheeseburgers, chilidogs, carrots, corn, cabbage, cottage fries, and chicken, I called it The Strictly C-Food Diet Plan.

And it's worked like a charm. My weight has scaled down and stayed within a reasonable range even though, according to my customized C-Food Plan, I can have my cake—and eat it, too.

Best of all, when I've been a really calorie-conscious good girl all day, lugged innumerable loads of laundry up and down stairs, done field work for Little League batting practice, and accomplished the zillion business-oriented tasks working motherhood requires, I can treat myself to the most delicious kind of C-Food on my personal "allowables" list: a diminutive, but oh, so delightful dab of anything . . . *chocolate*.

Second Childhood

*A*t times, I wish I were a kid again. Those were the days when I could listen to different drummers. Lead, not follow. Believed I could do anything if I wanted it badly enough, including flying like Superman via a garage-roof launch.

Funny how those philosophies have changed.

As a body-conscious grown-up, I climb aboard every new diet and iron-pumping bandwagon just to fit fashion's whim. A pear cannot an hourglass become, but I try and try again.

But if I were a kid again, I'd measure the same from sternum to stern—vital statistics I failed to appreciate while they lasted. And to heck with a designer's idea of de rigueur duds—I'd pull on a purple sweatshirt, orange-and-green-striped pants, and red polka-dotted socks if that combination struck my fancy. Come to think of it, I think a Parisian couturier was promoting that ensemble last fall.

This discriminating adult would think twice before remodeling a room unless a decorator agreed my chosen slices of a color wheel's pie promised a superior interior. God forbid I should risk committing a country French faux pas.

But if I were a kid again, I'd fill my room with precious collectibles called My Stuff and how it looked to anyone else wouldn't matter one whit. Not with Oreos stashed in a shoe box, a diary tucked in my underwear drawer, and magazine-page photos of my favorite movie stars and singers Scotch taped to the walls.

Leaving my pajamas lying on the floor, the bed unmade, and letting a warm, purry cat shed all over the sheets would be more standard operating procedure than sin.

Occasionally, I socialize with people I don't particularly like because as a grown-up, I know that *what* I know isn't always as important as *whom* I know. So, I chit and chat and nibble potentially ptomainic tidbits such as bacon-wrapped animal entrails simply because the host/hostess insists that culinary respects be paid to those pricey renderings.

But if I were a kid again, I would mind my manners during social situations, but I wouldn't be expected to converse beyond mumbled monosyllables. As for my peers, I'd still prefer popularity to solidarity, but whiners, braggarts, and tattle-tales wouldn't be tolerated for long. Who'd need *them*, with beloved stuffed animals at my beck and bawl and a best friend to take turns spending the night with every Friday after school?

If I were a kid again, I could get away with saying "Yuck" when that hors d'oeuvre tray was passed. In fact, the hostess would probably chuckle and send me to the kitchen for a peanut-butter-and-cracker feast.

During family dinners, foods I didn't like or didn't like the looks of wouldn't rate a taste either. Oh, I'd act like I had just to avoid hearing about all those starving Chinese children again, but then I'd sneaker the stuff behind a table leg for the dog to find.

Except I am an adult, so I work myself to exhaustion, both domestically and professionally, to achieve an indefinable goal known as Having It All. Yet I can't help wondering, if I ever got It, would I be able to tell I had It, and if so, where would I go from there?

But if I were a kid again, I'd be "forced" to go outside and play in the sunshine for my own good. And I'd be deemed too little to scrape an icy windshield, mow the lawn, or even *stand* near a hot stove.

It would be okay to sleep with the light on—especially on stormy nights. And if I kicked the covers off, somebody'd notice, tuck me in again, gently kiss my sleep-warm cheek, and whisper, "Sweet dreams, honey."

Better yet, I'd be made to take a nap when I looked tired and if I didn't feel well, a 7-Up or a cherry Popsicle would be brought to my bedside. Curling up under an afghan with a good book would be applauded, not perceived as a guilty "should"—time I *should* be devoting to more worthwhile deeds.

If I were a kid again, there'd be galaxies of bright and shining What Will Bes to wish upon. I'd dream of do-anything-I-want tomorrows when I'd be an adult and not dependent on anyone. The future would stretch like a ball of soft taffy: warm, sweet, and infinitely flexible.

Except I *am* grown up, and sometimes I catch myself wishing upon the star of What Was; cherishing the remembrance of days when it was okay to fail, okay to cry, okay not to know any better, okay to be afraid of inexplicable things that probably don't exist, and okay to *want* to be taken care of sometimes.

When I *was* a kid, those wet-behind-the-ears years seemed much like measles: something to be gotten over as quickly as possible.

But now, how I *wish* I could catch that youthful affliction again. Of course, if I did, how differently it would be diagnosed. A midlife crisis, other grown-ups might call it . . .

> *Star light, star bright,*
> *I'm gonna wish on a star tonight,*
> *I wish I may, I wish I might,*
> *So eat my dust and hang on tight,*
> *'Cause it's never too late for a second childhood . . .*
> *Right?*